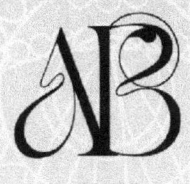

THIS COLORING BOOK BELONGS TO:

_____

Copyright © 2022 A.B.

All rights reserved. No part of this work may be reproduced or utilized in any form or by any means, electronic or mechanical, including photocopying, recording, or by any information storage-and-retrieval system, without the prior written permission of the publisher.

Inner Peace and Inspiration

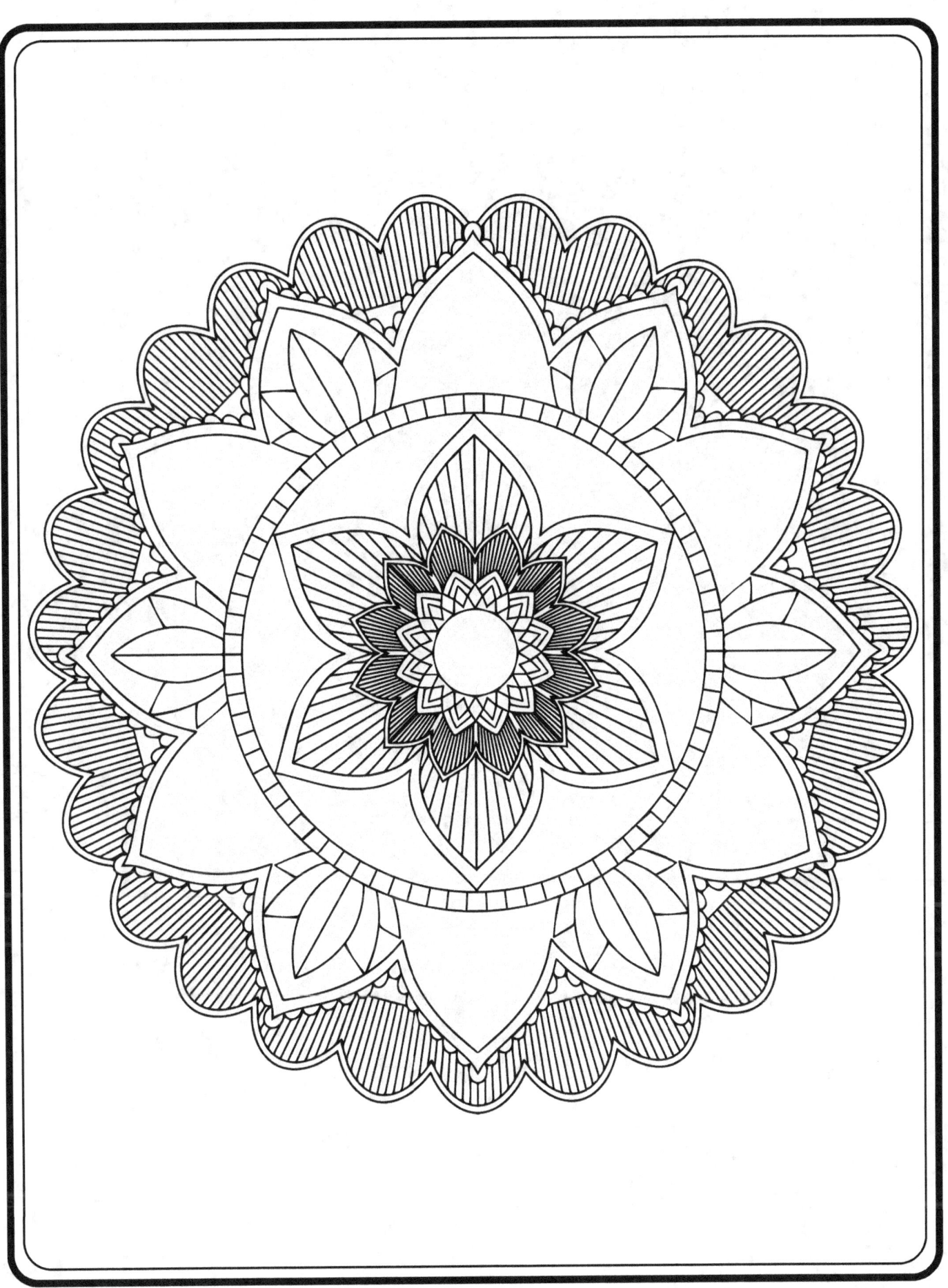

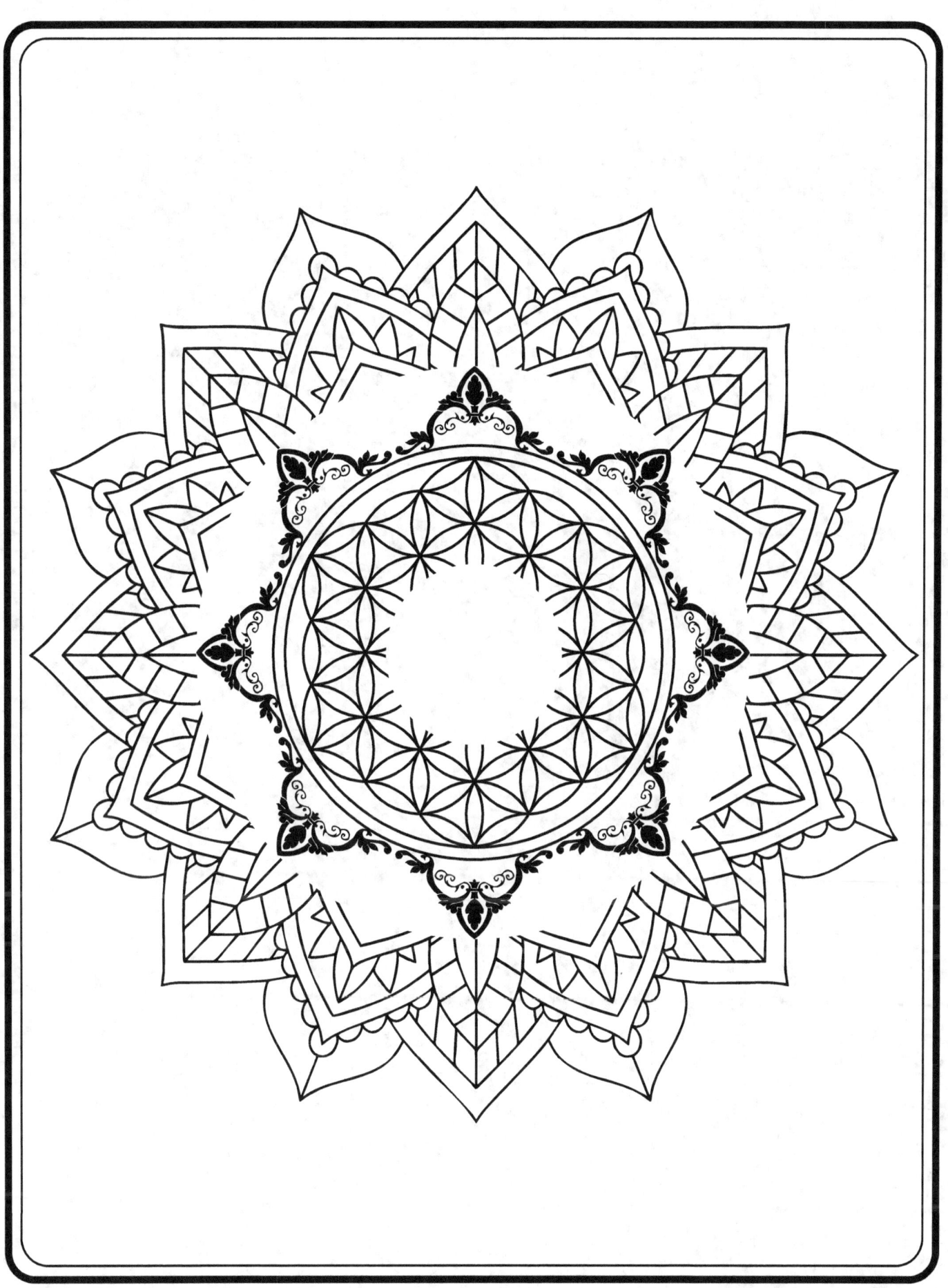

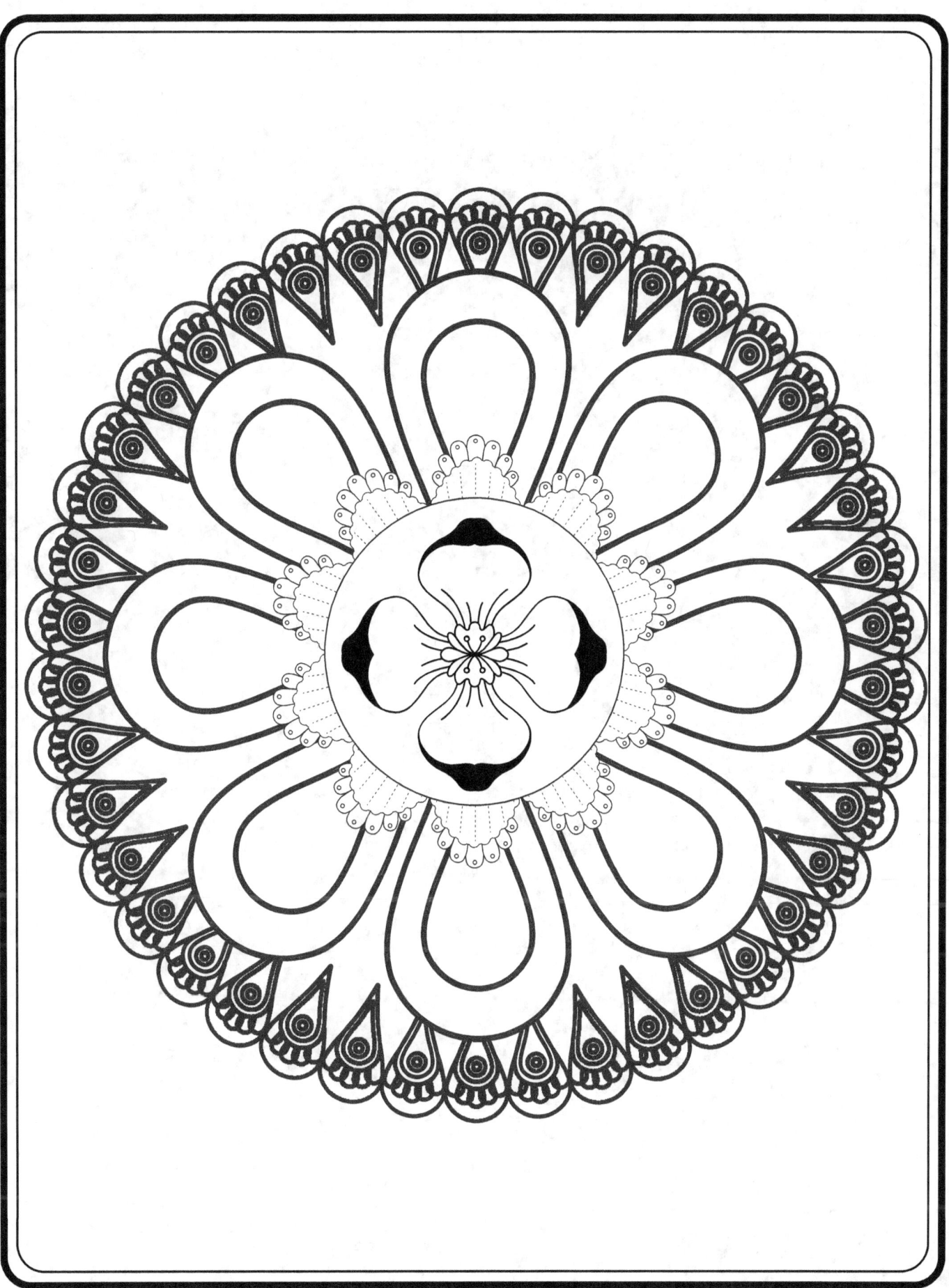

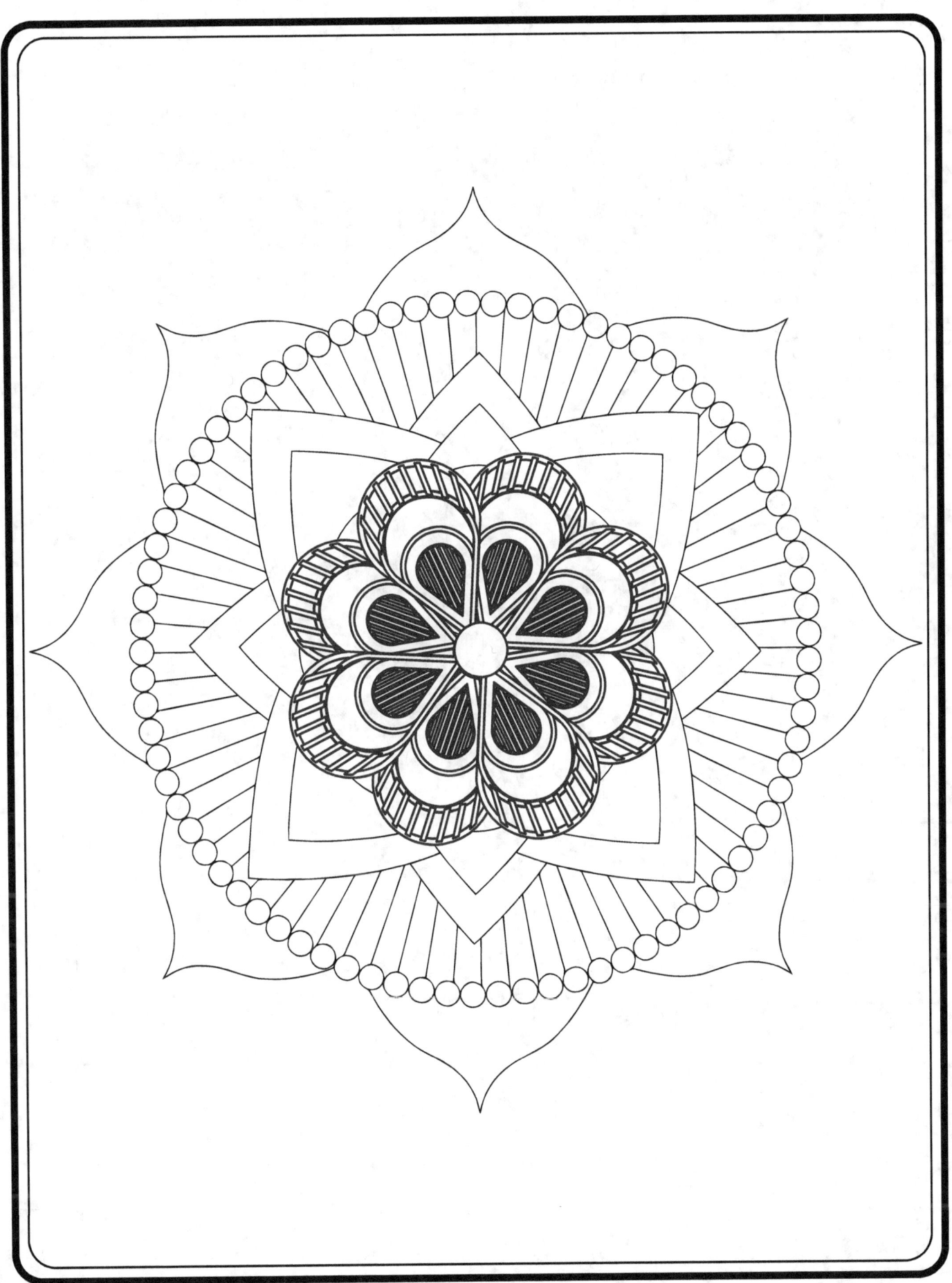

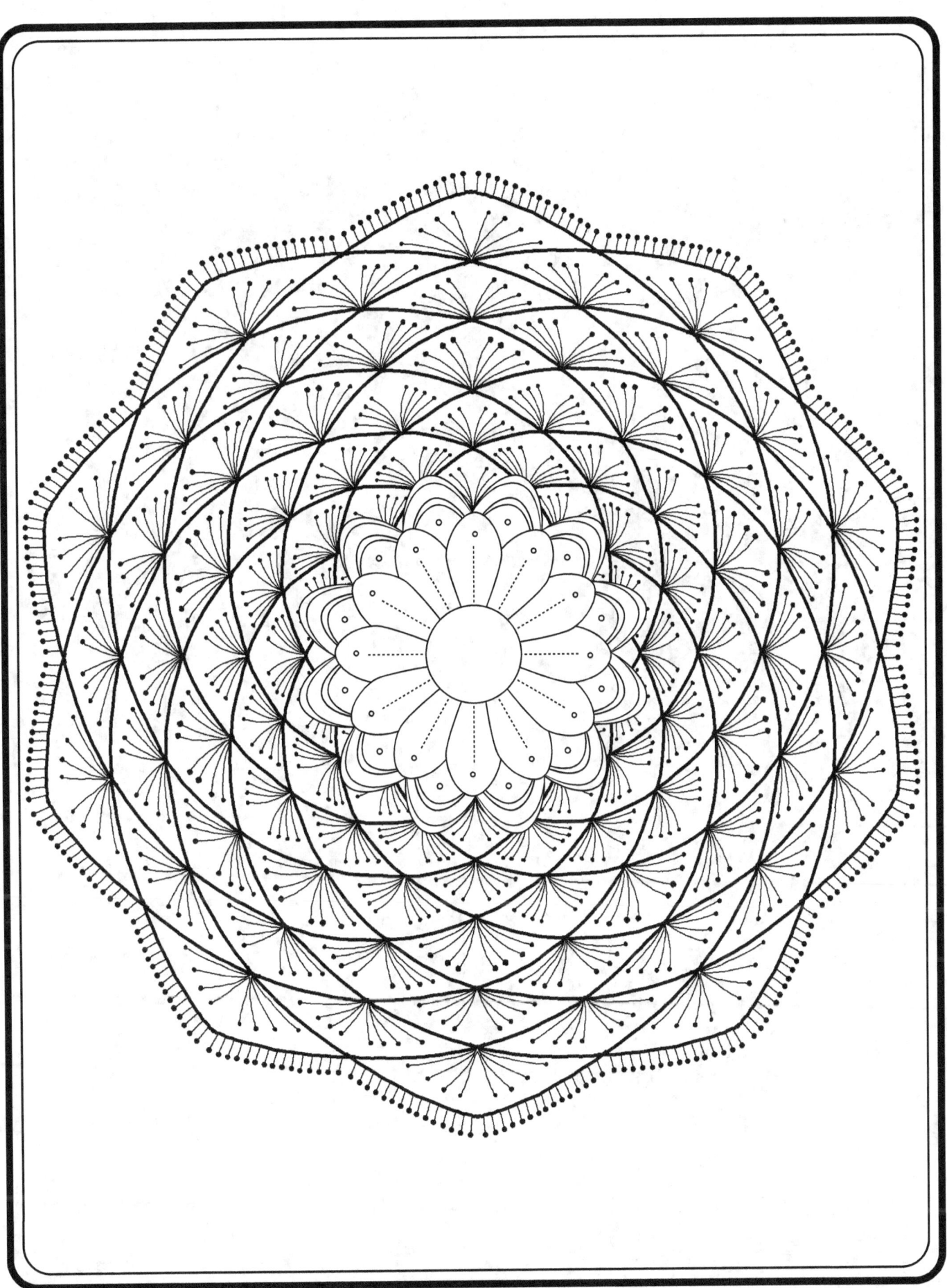

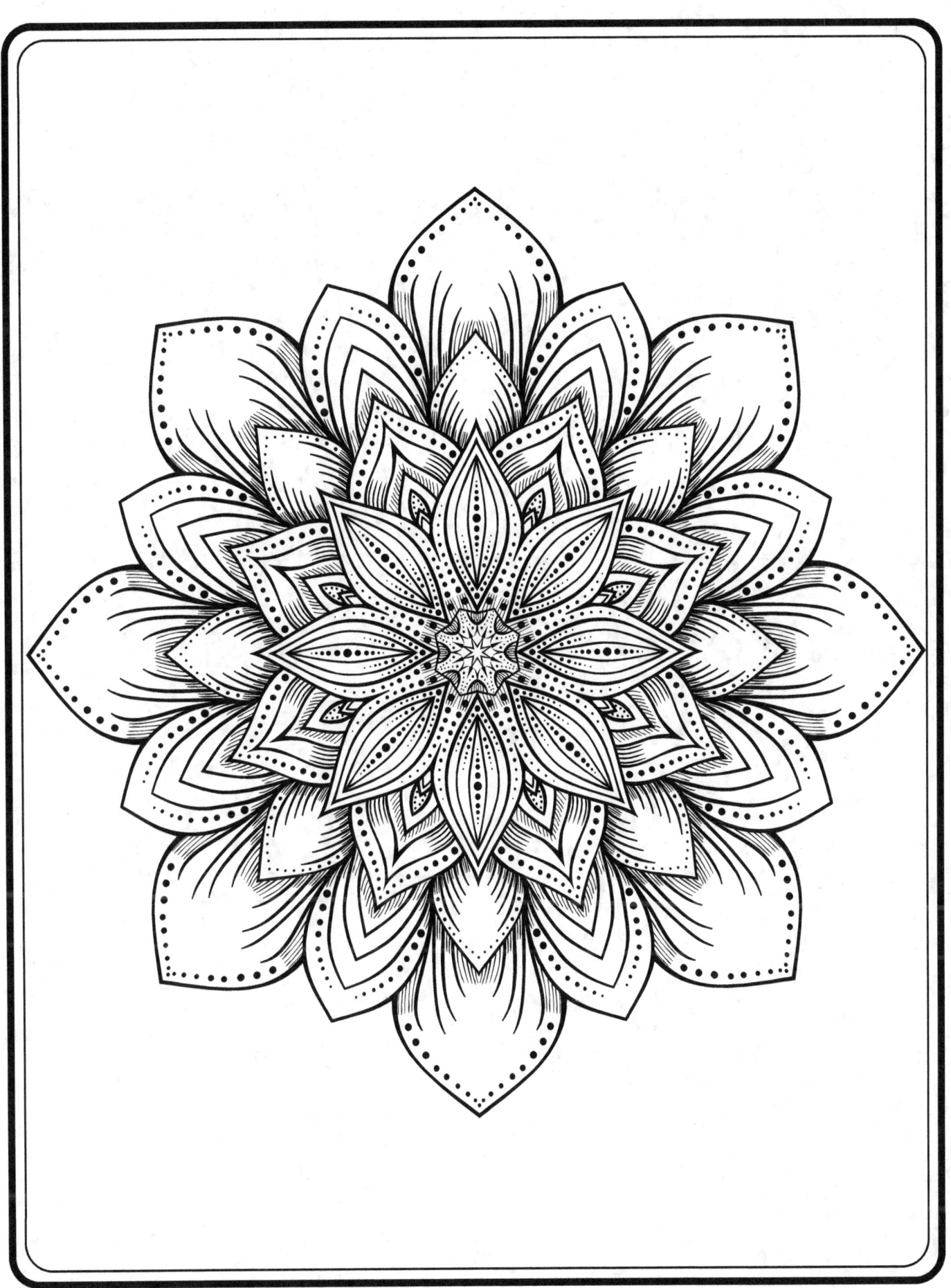

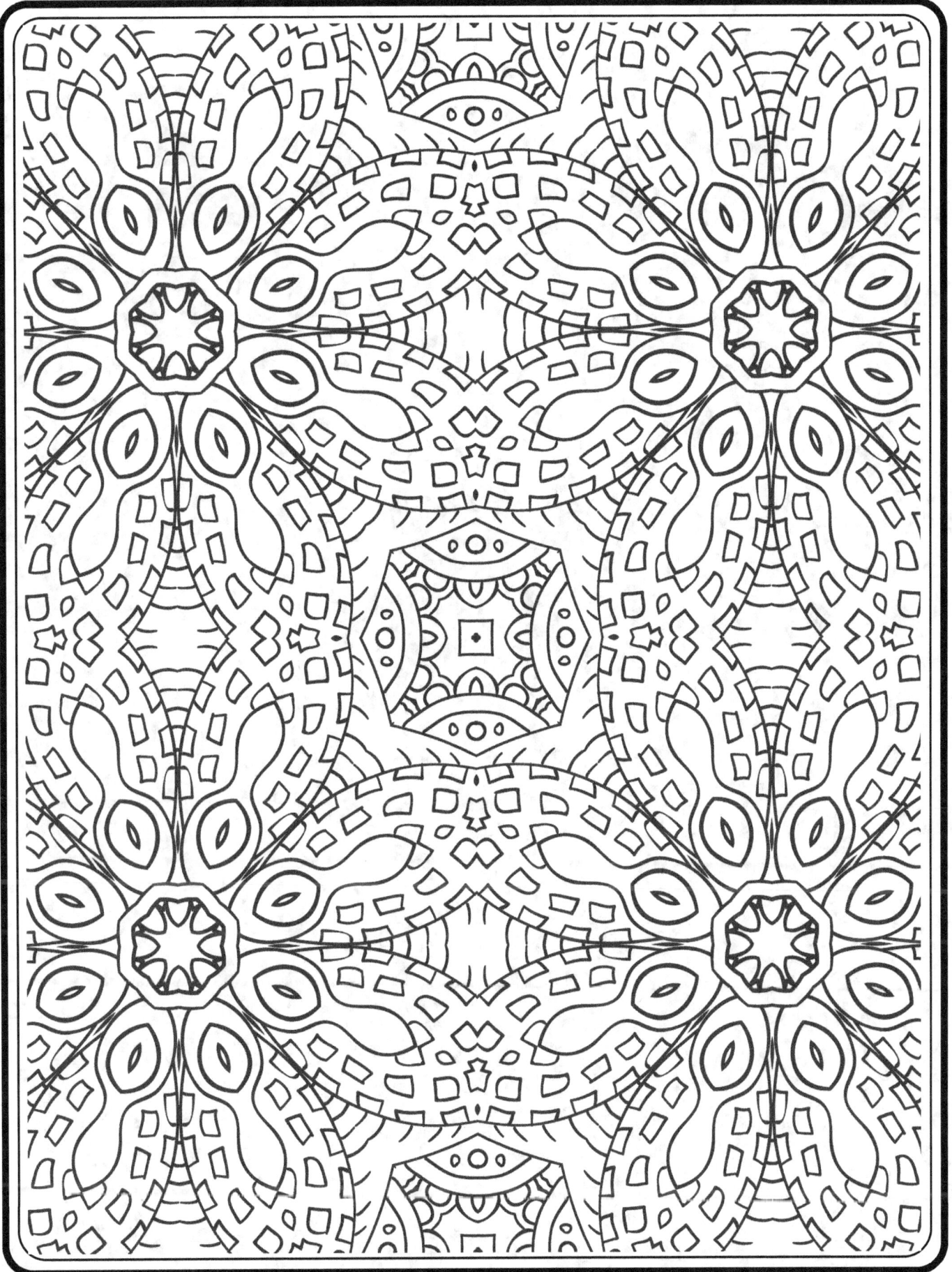

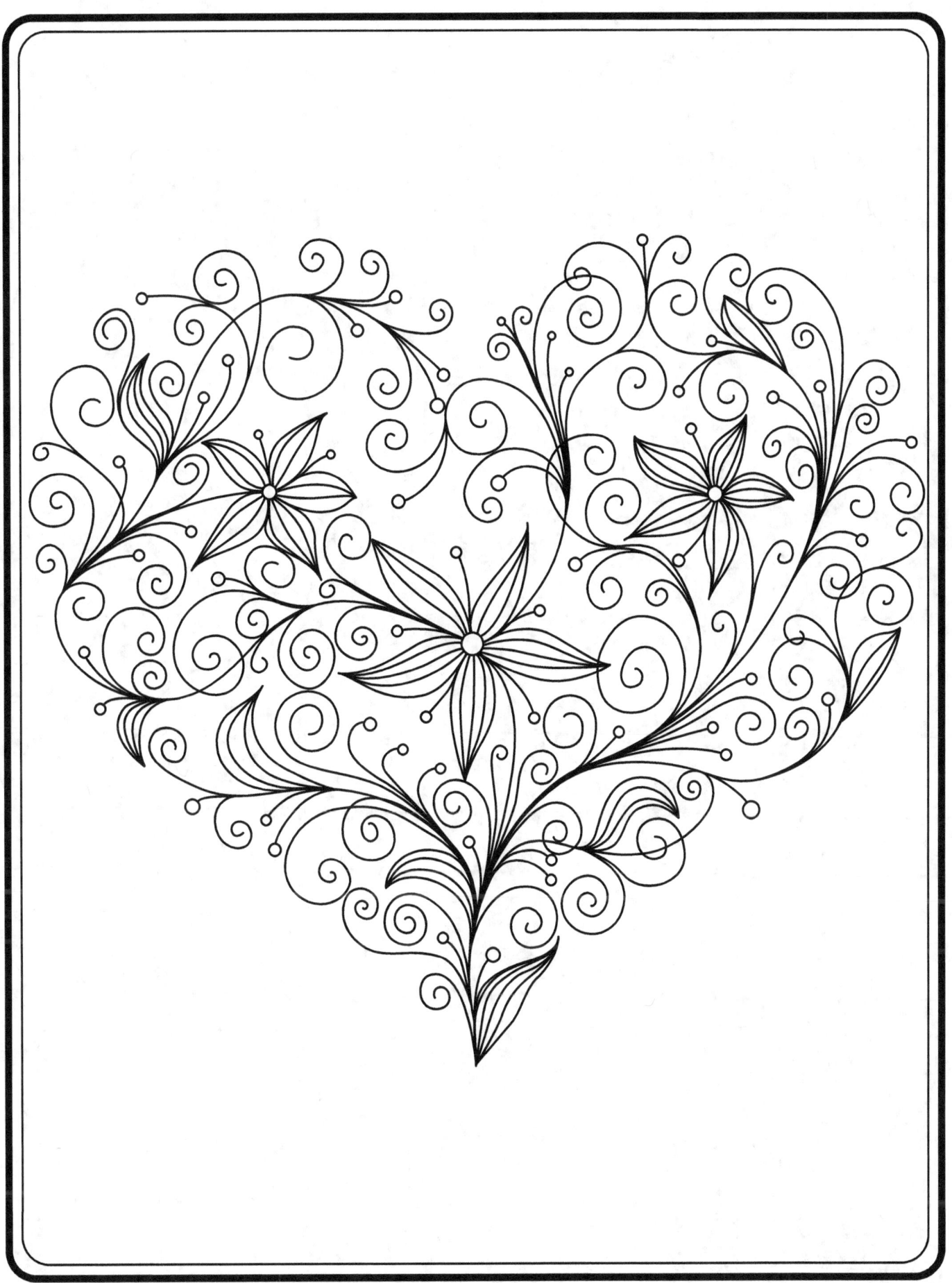

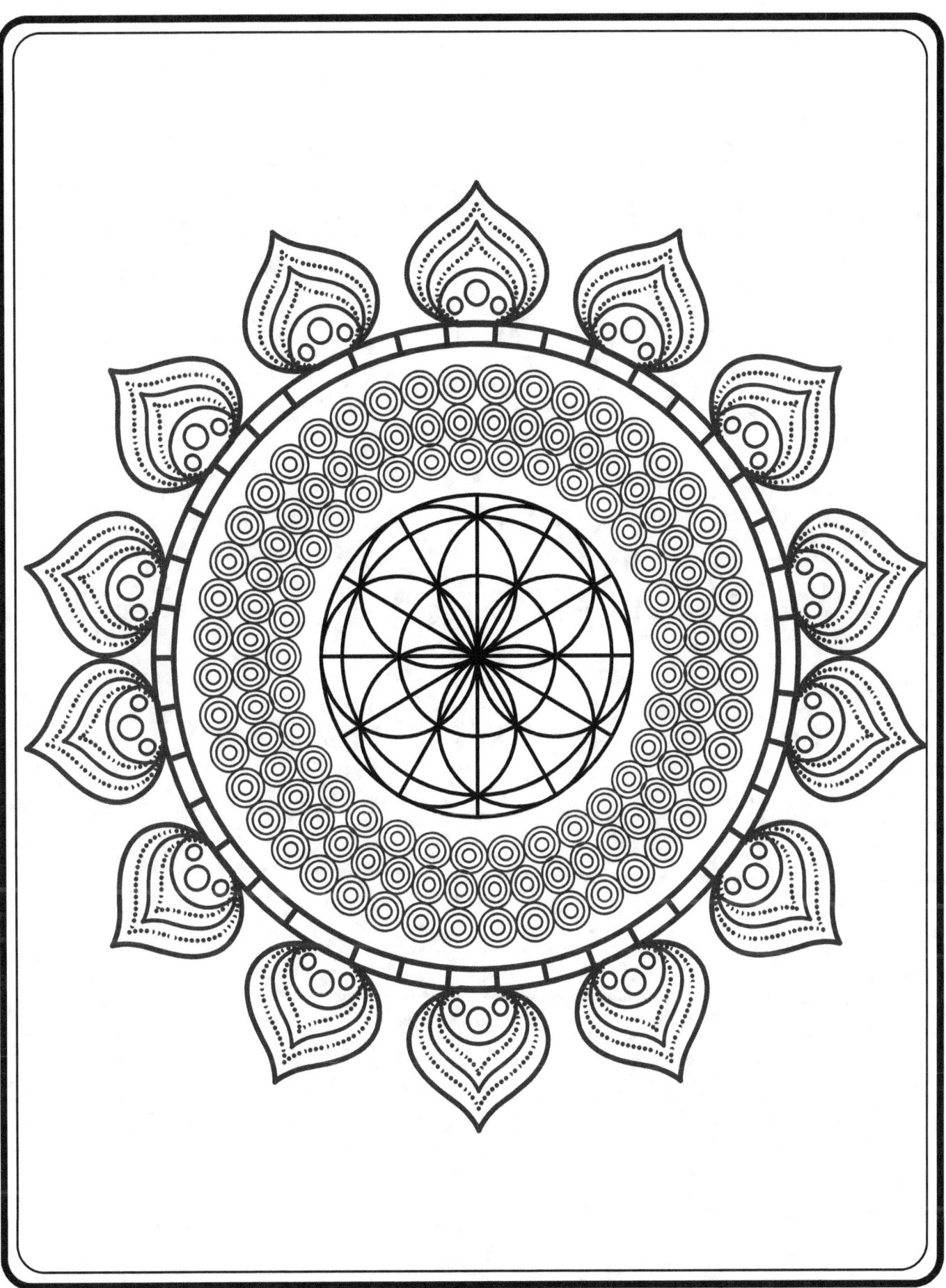

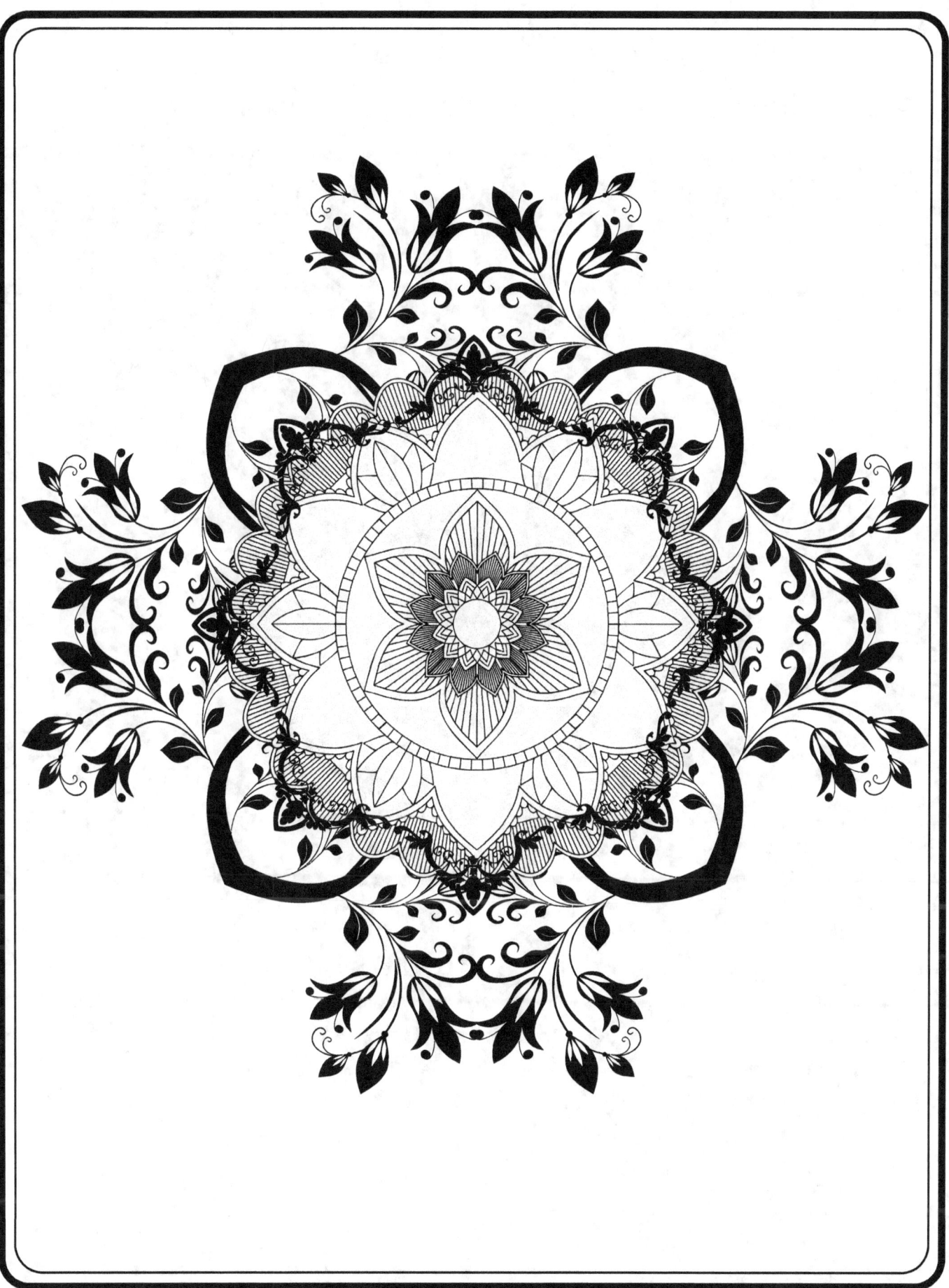

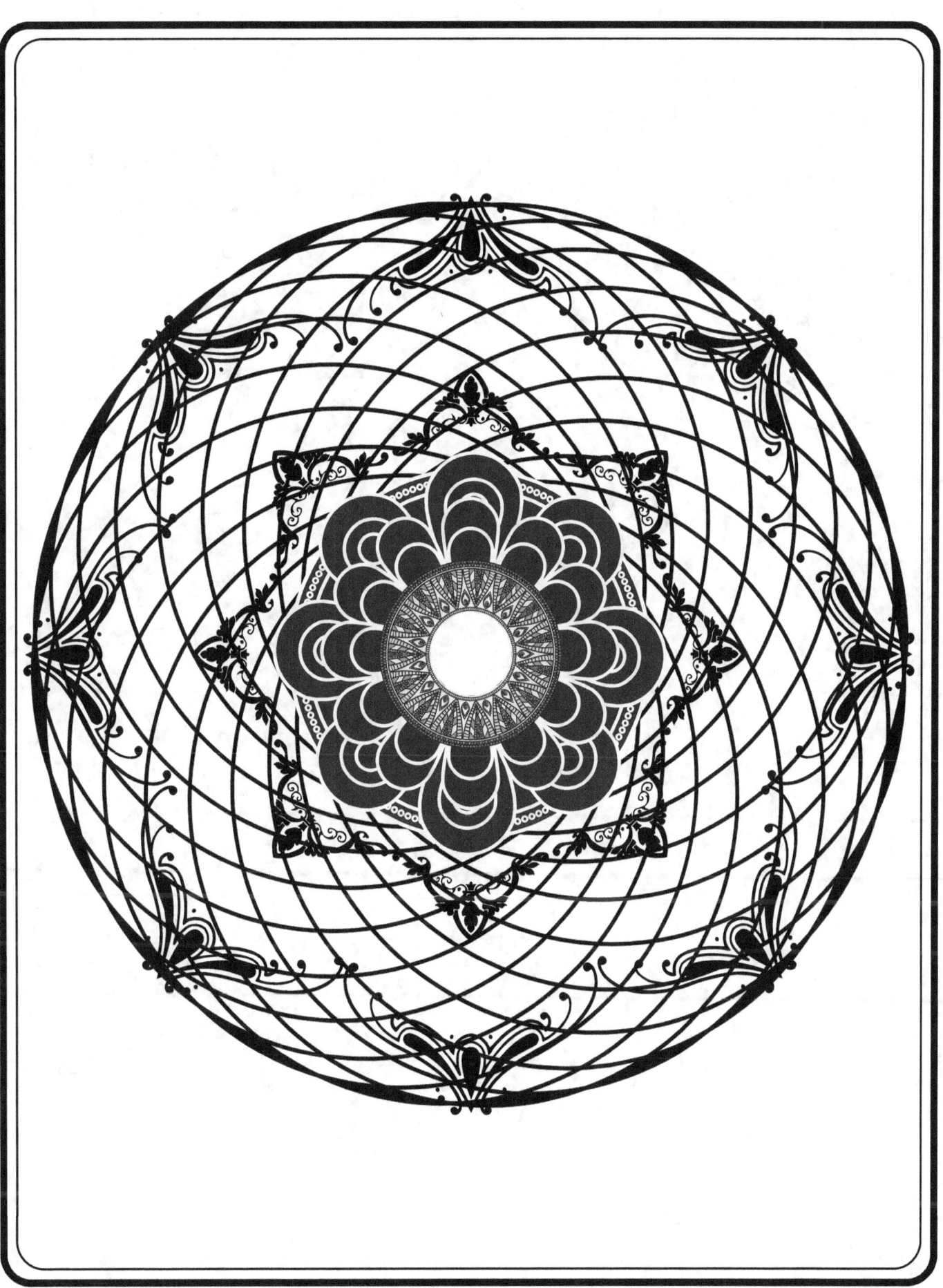

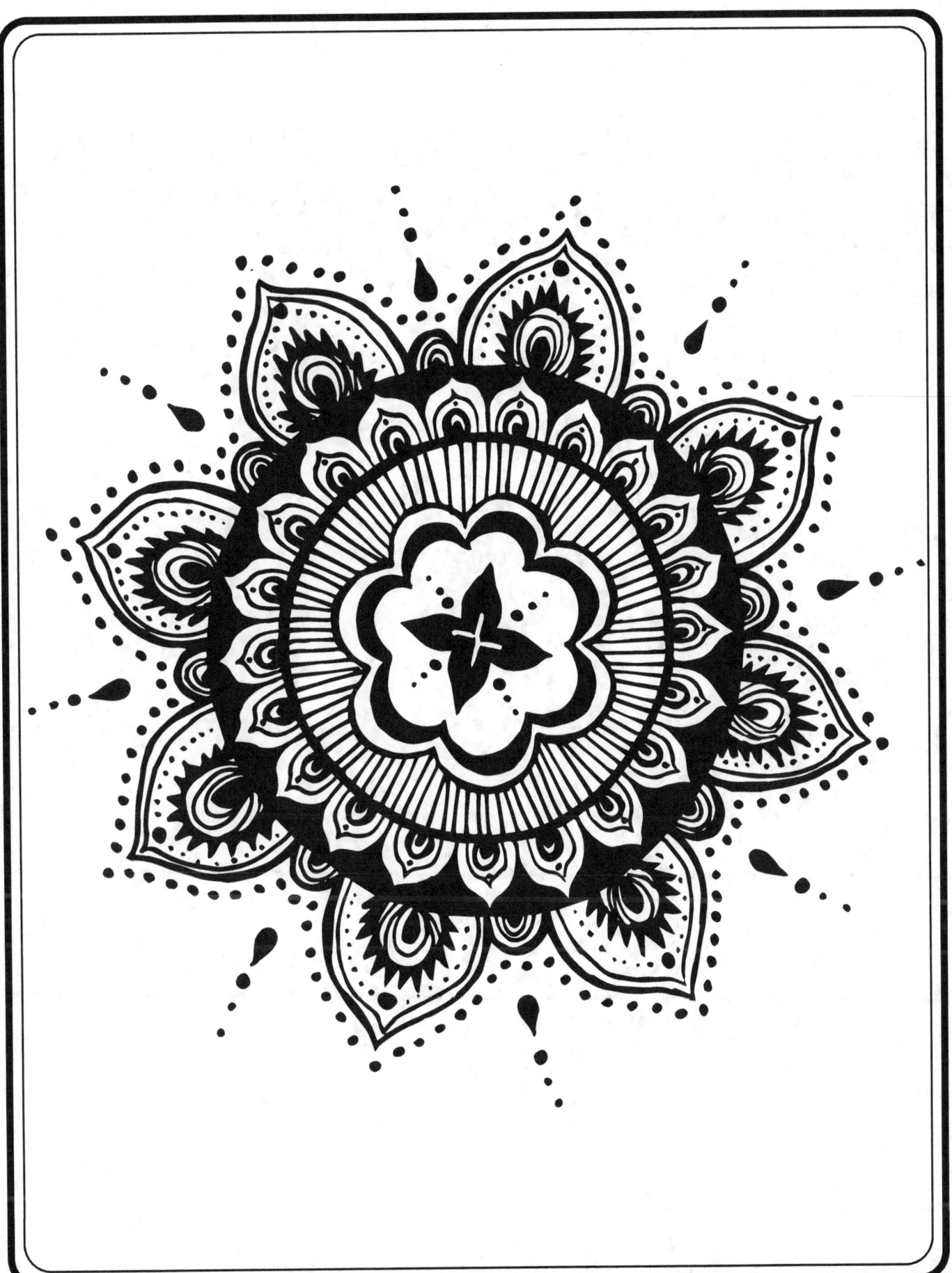

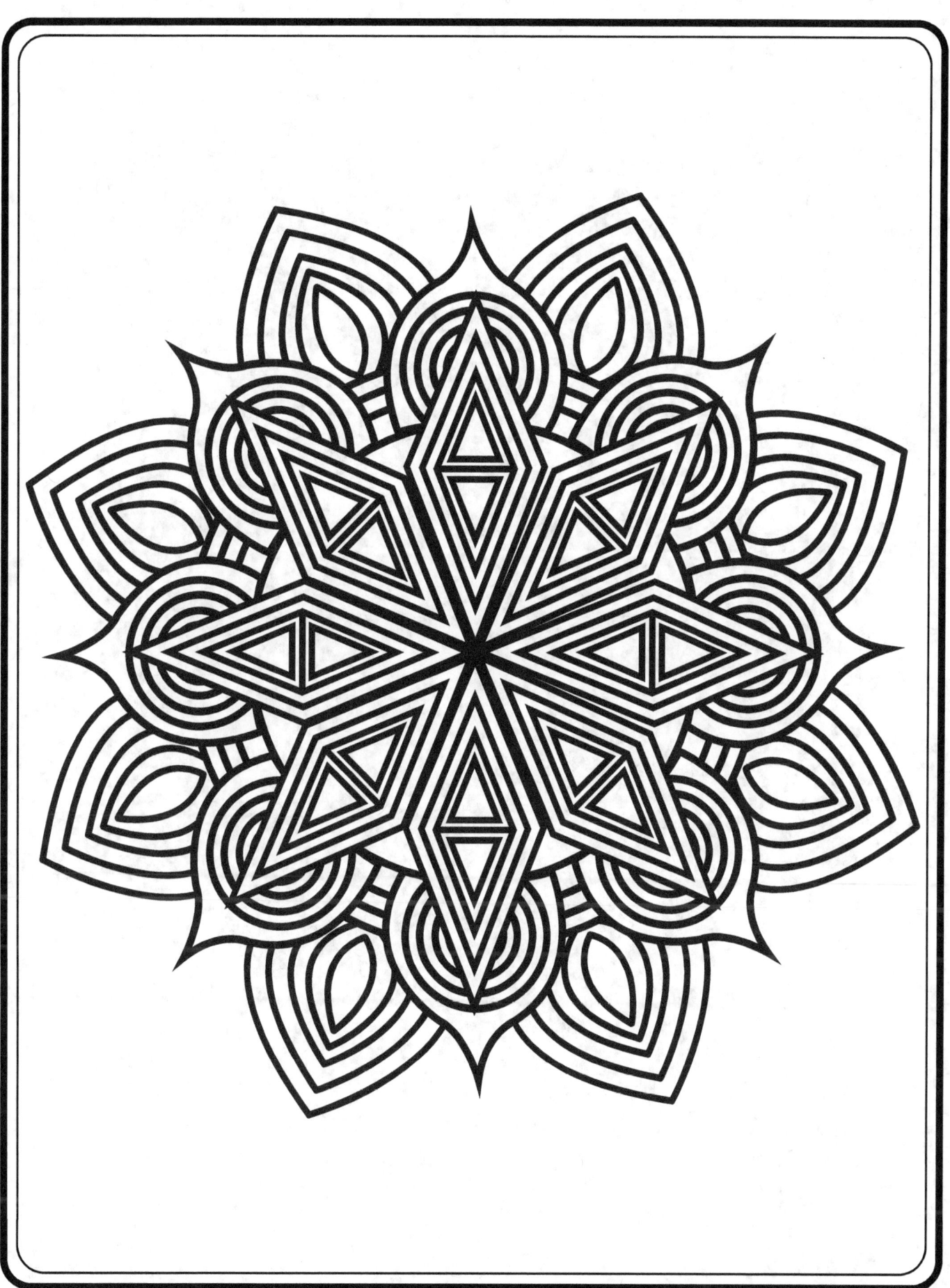

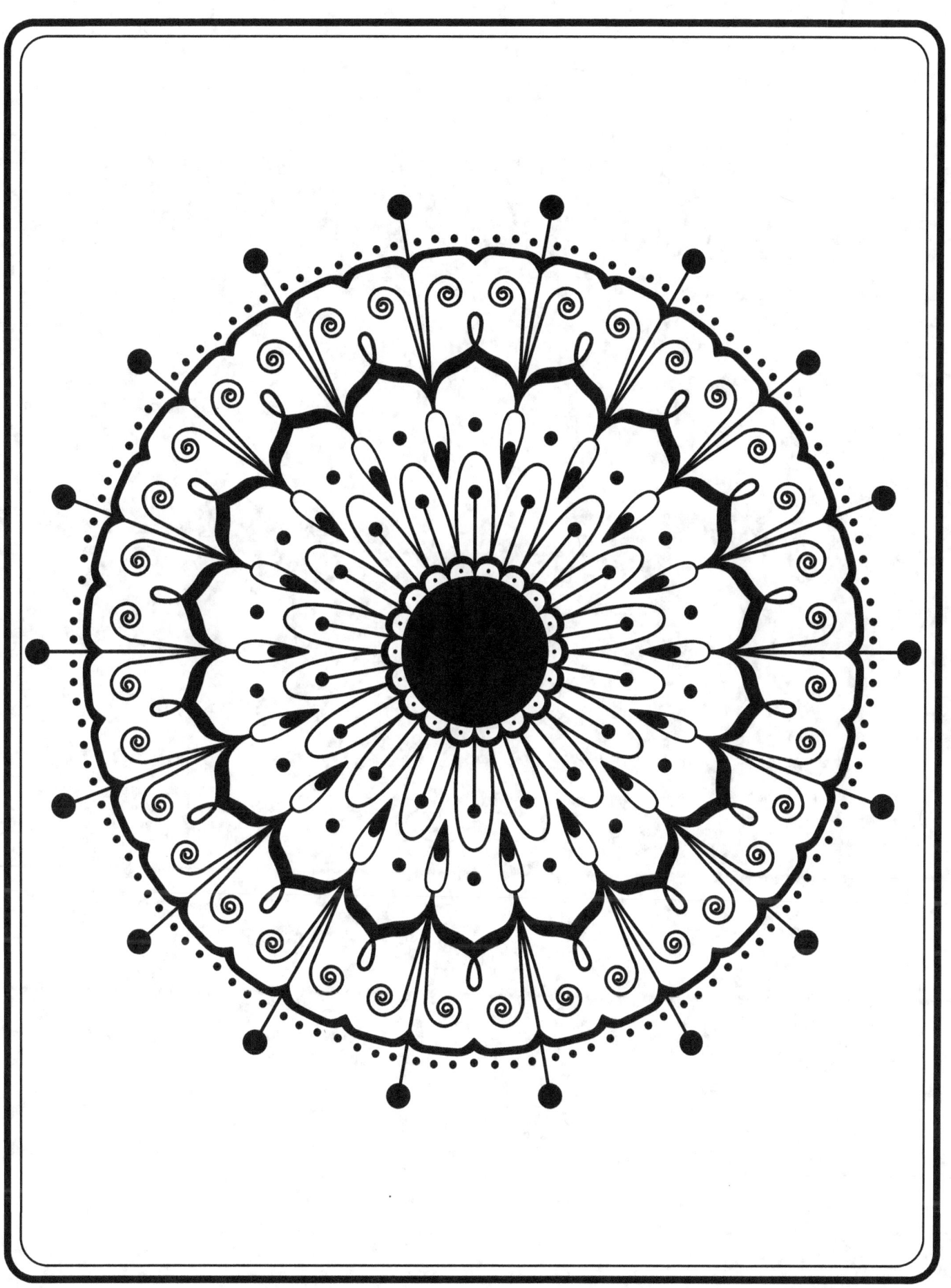

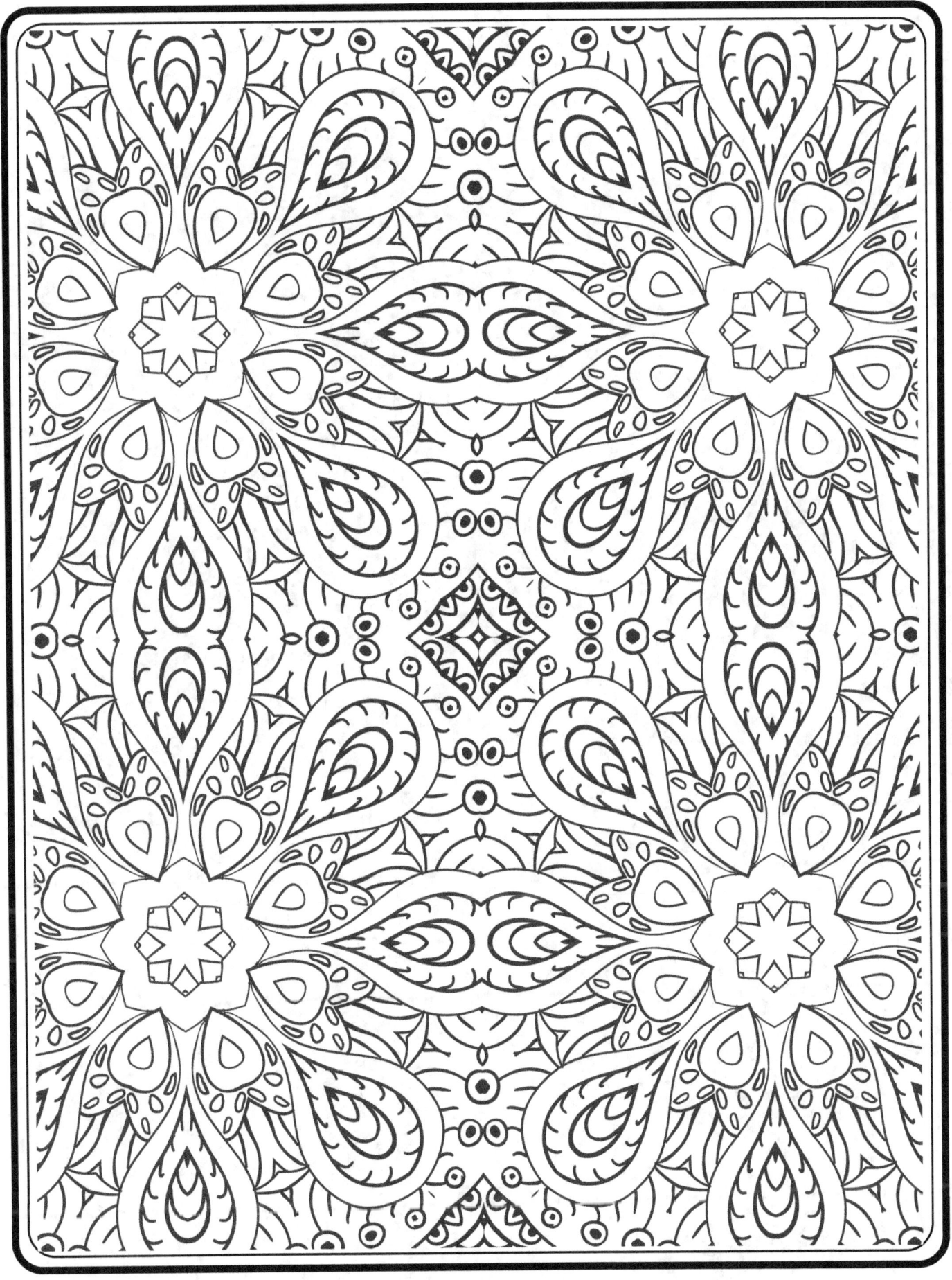

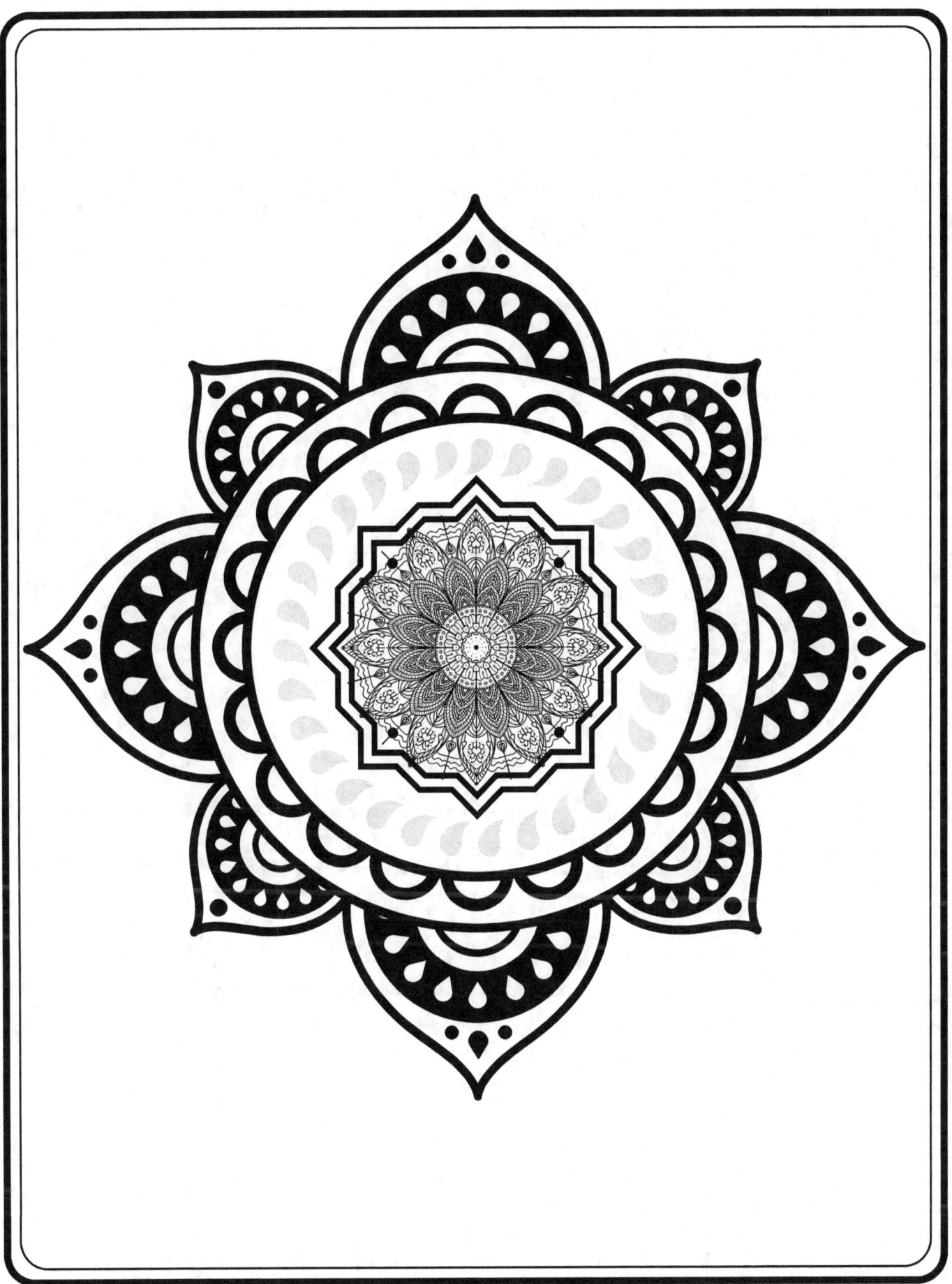

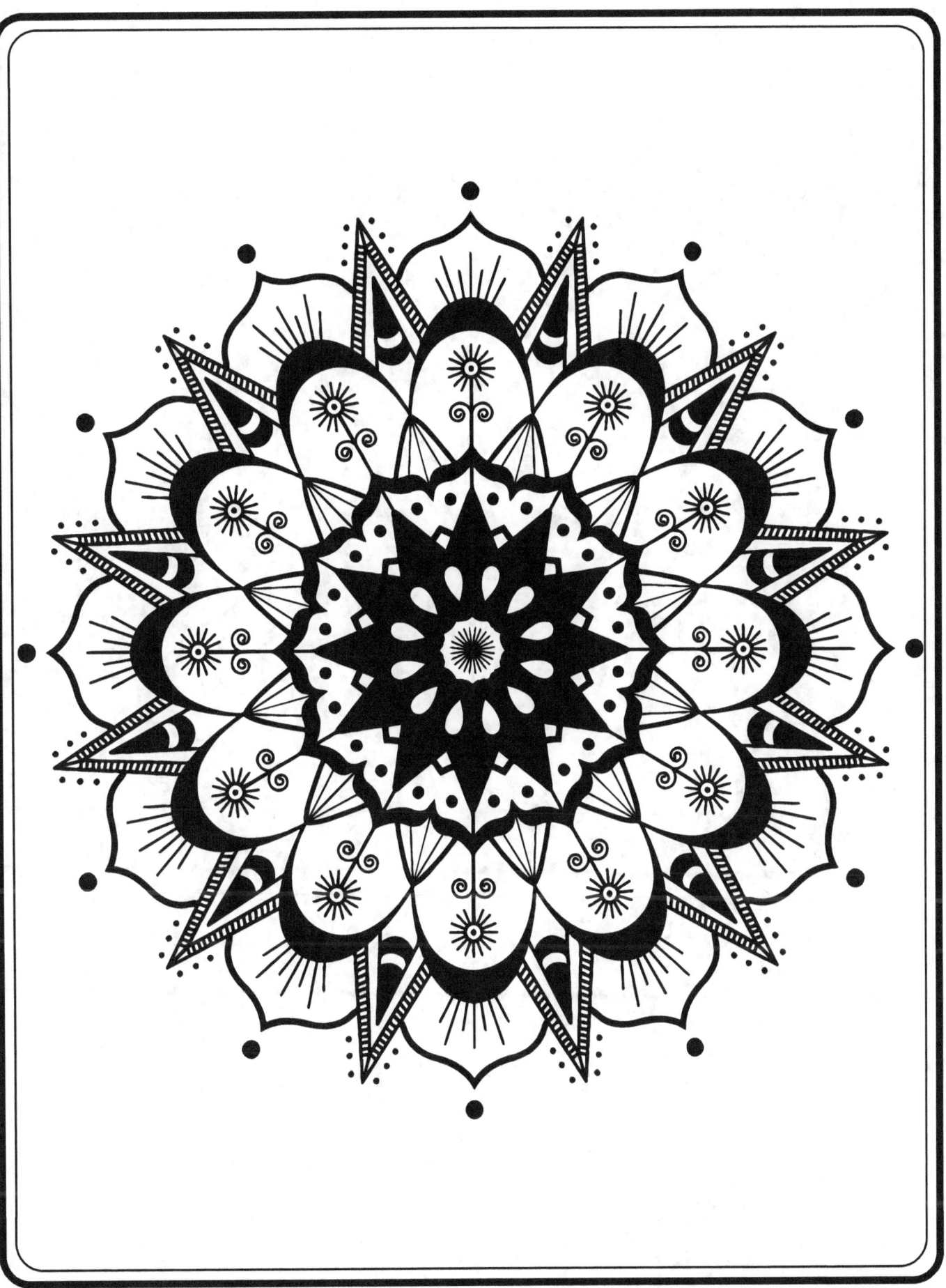

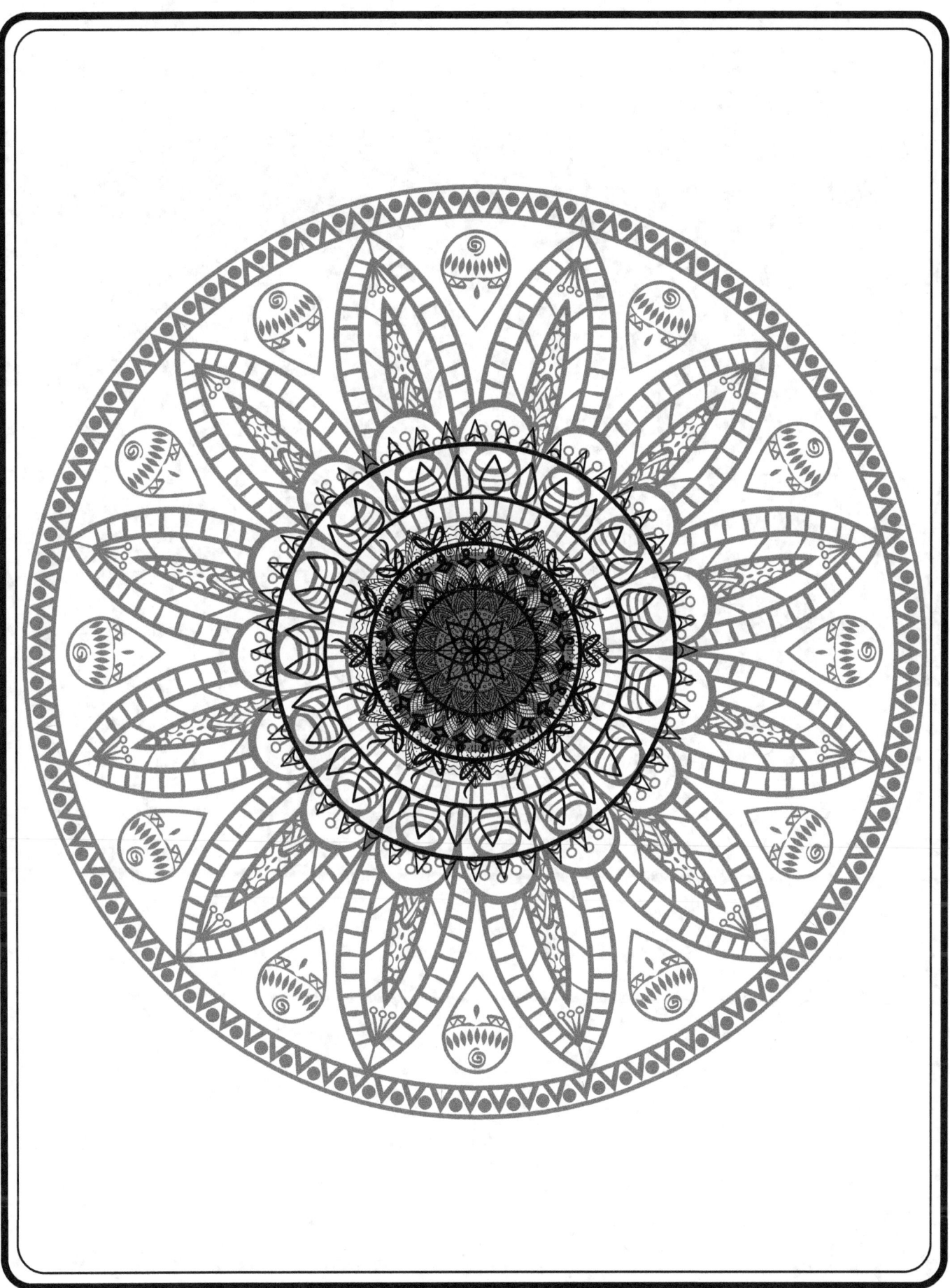

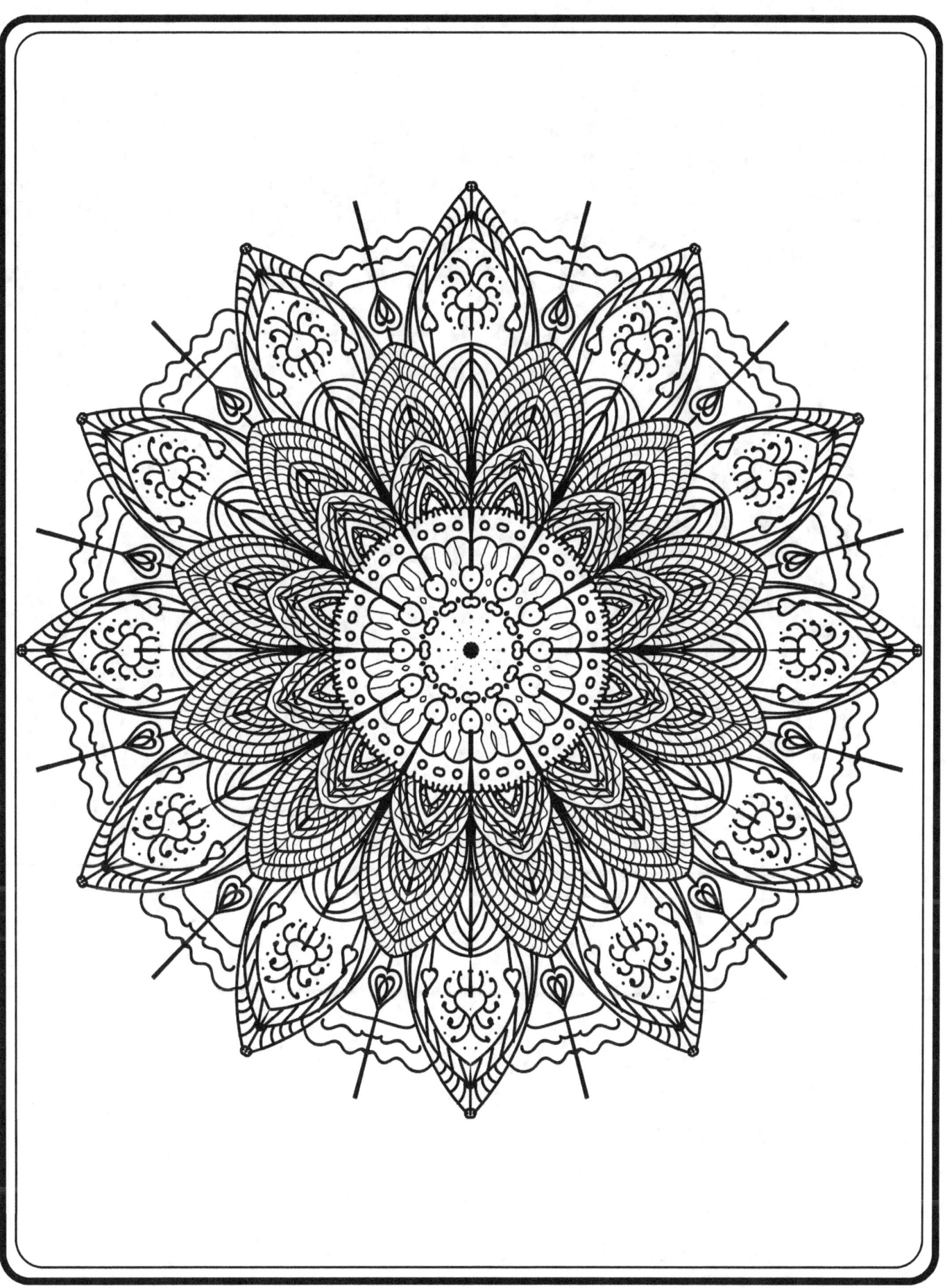

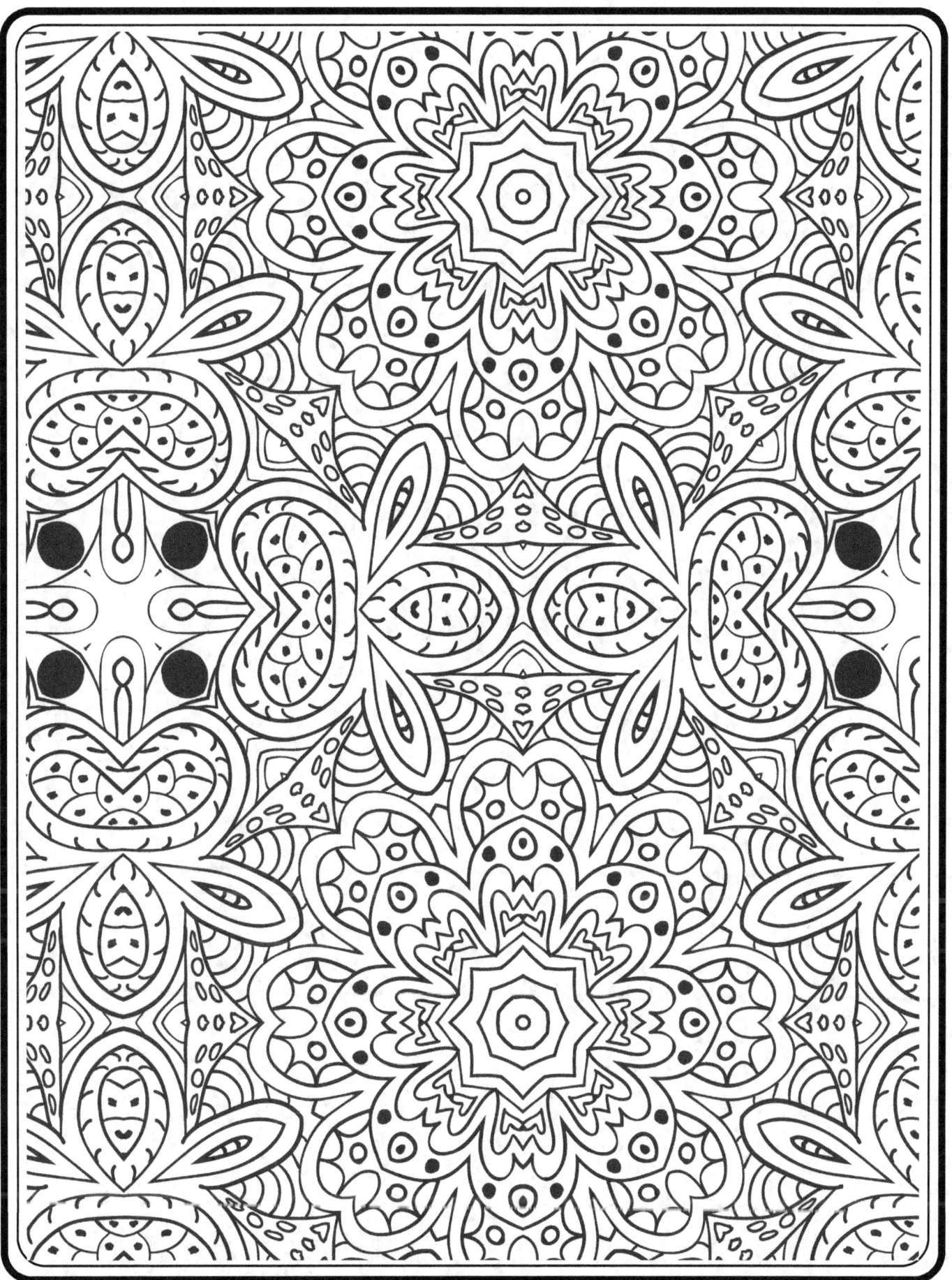

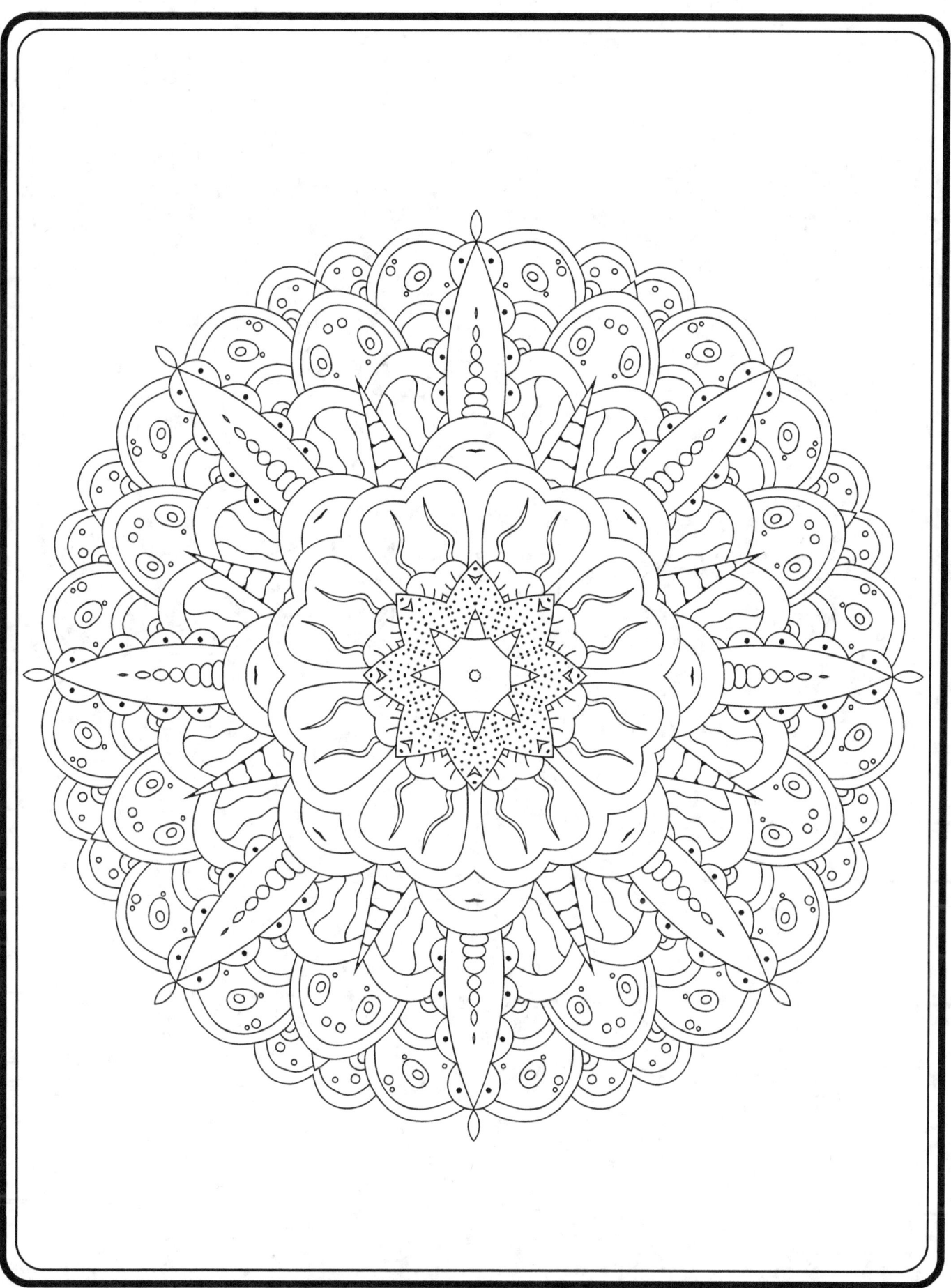

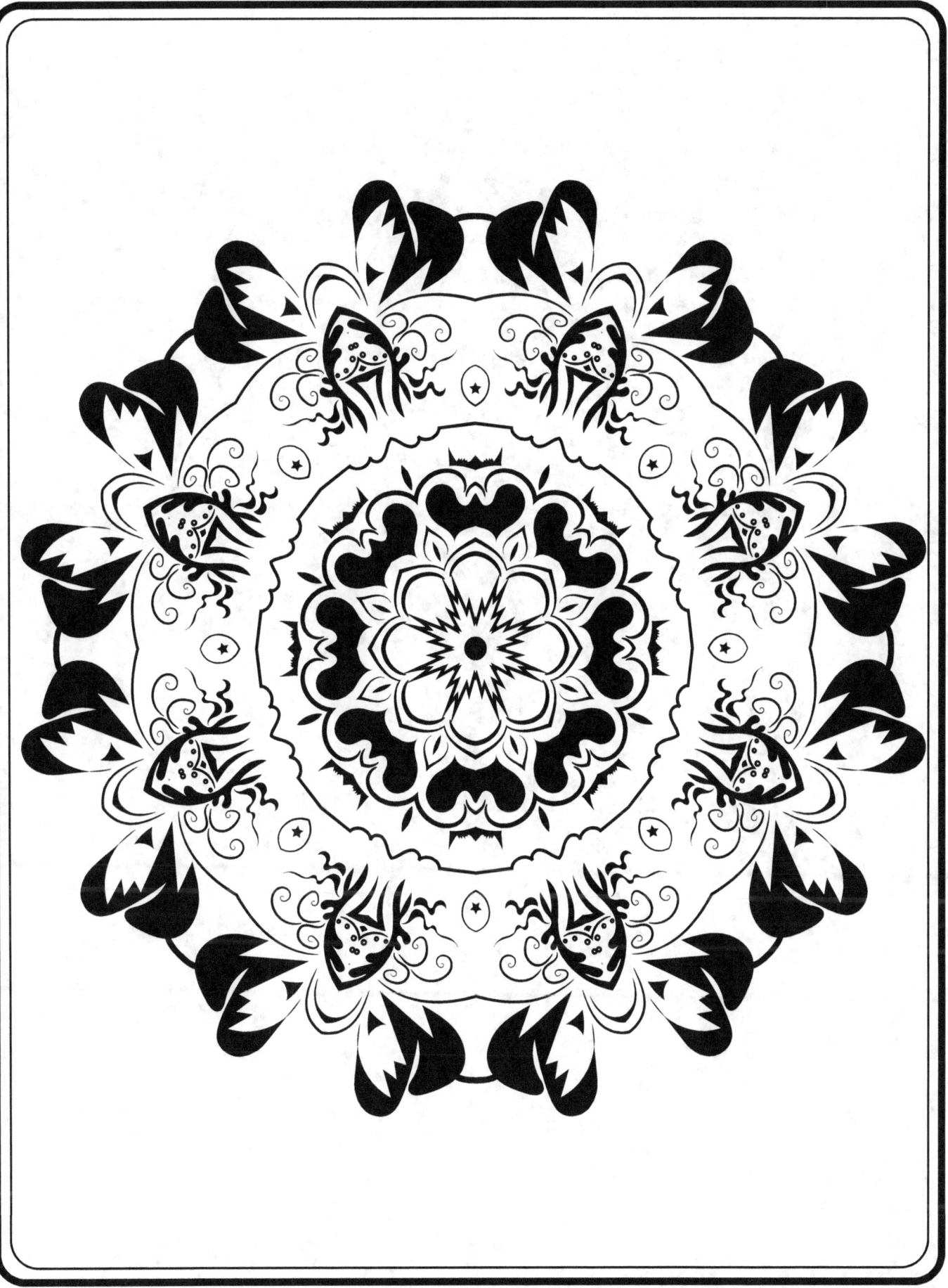

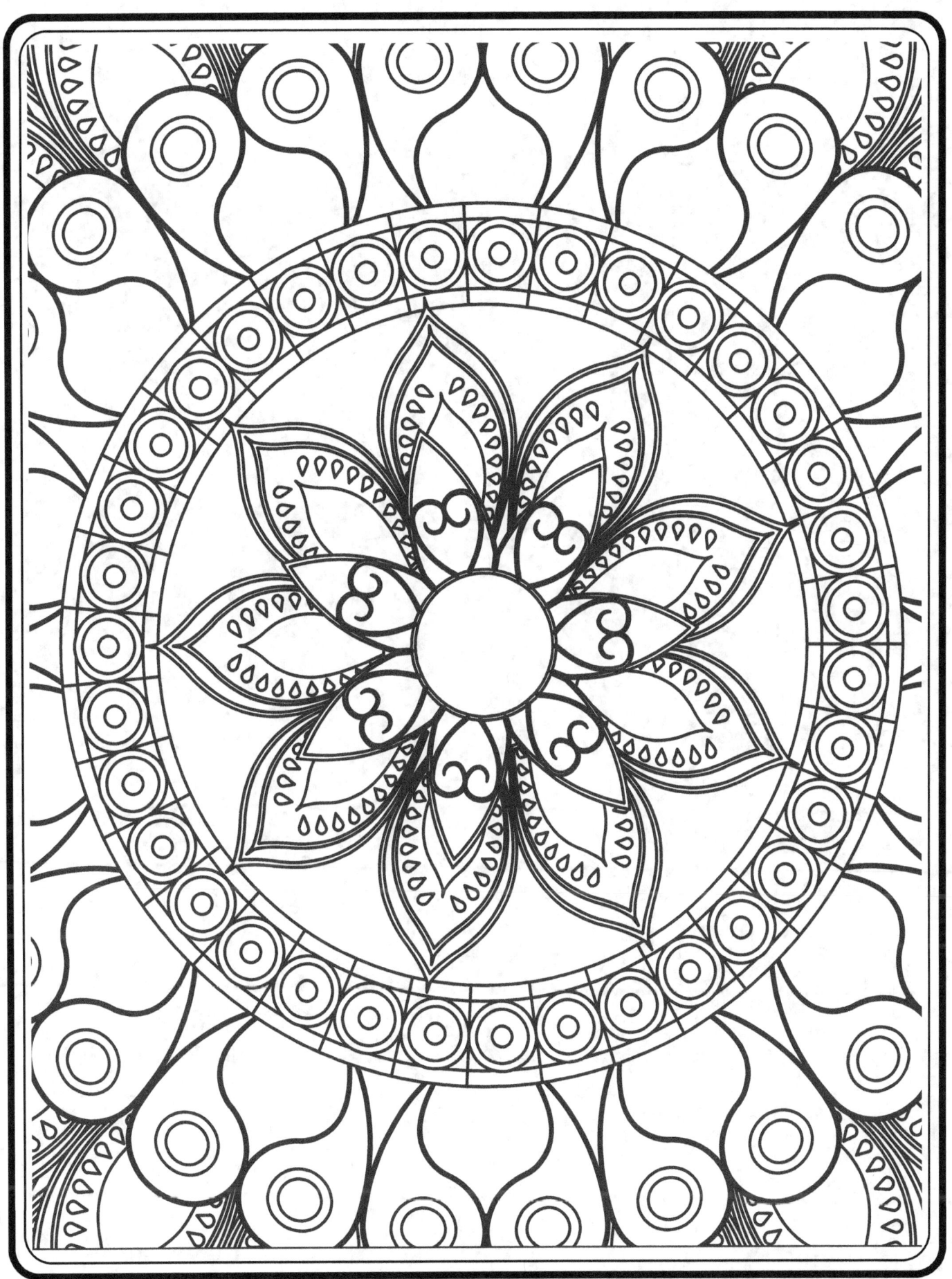

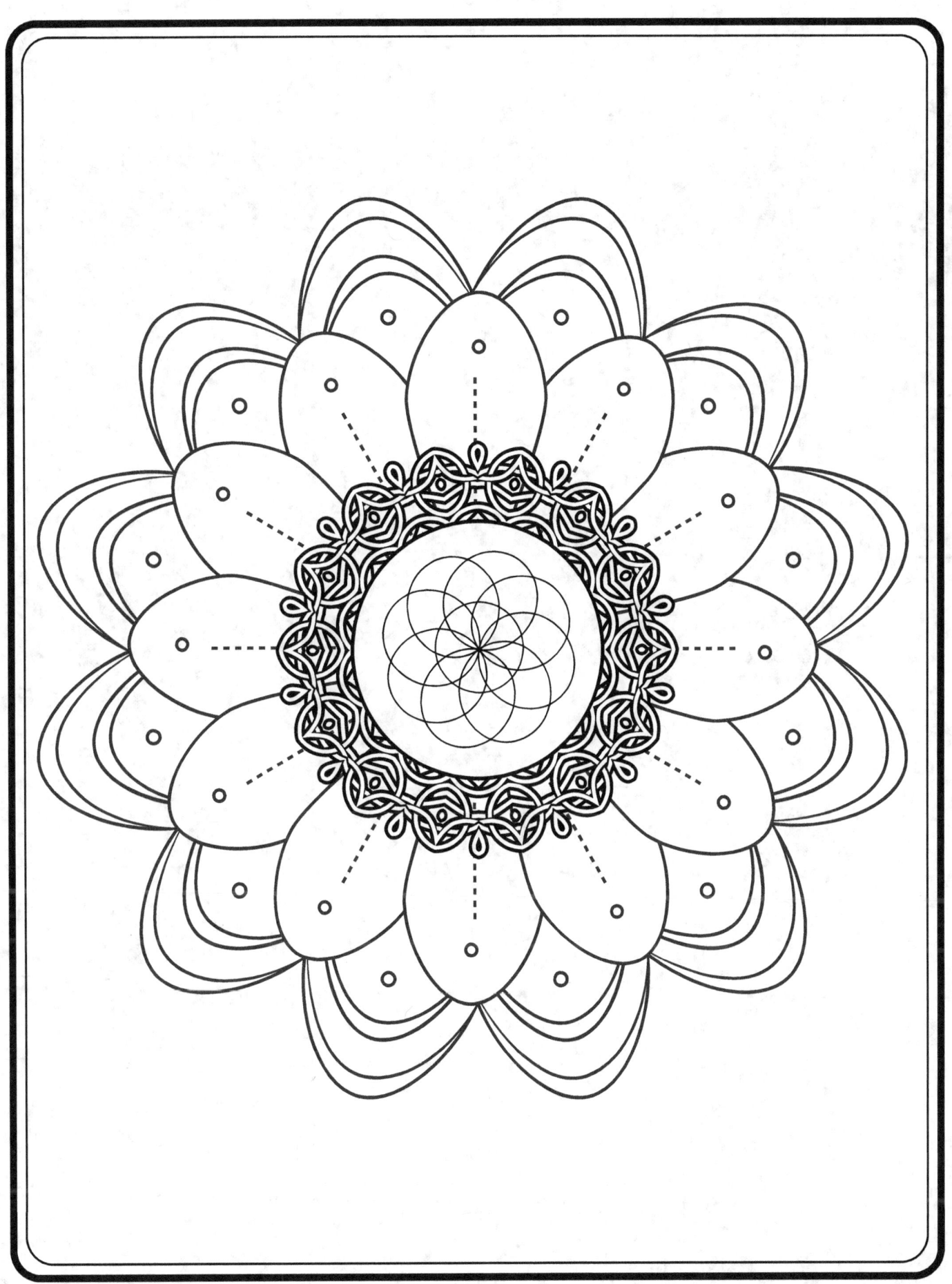

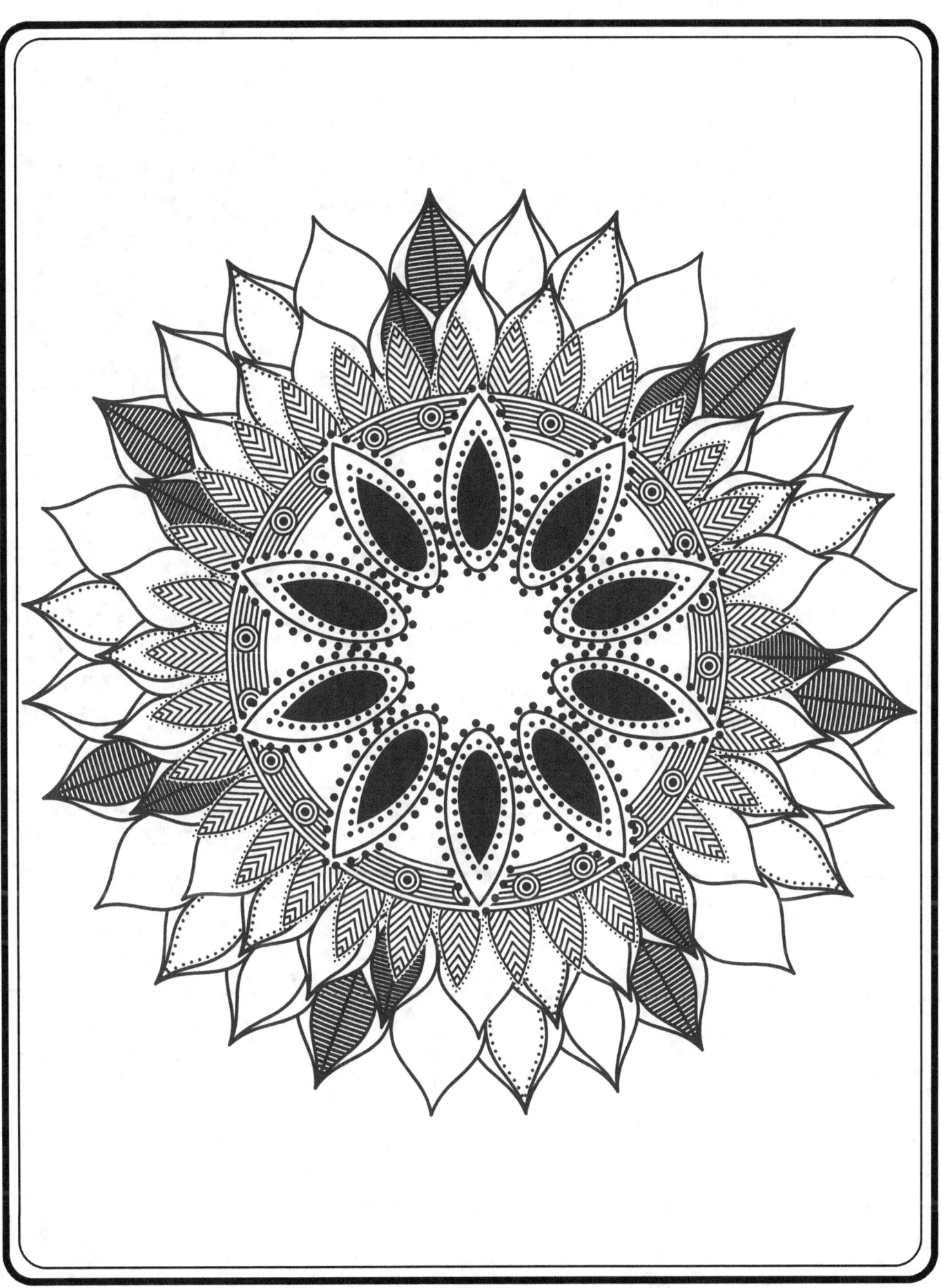

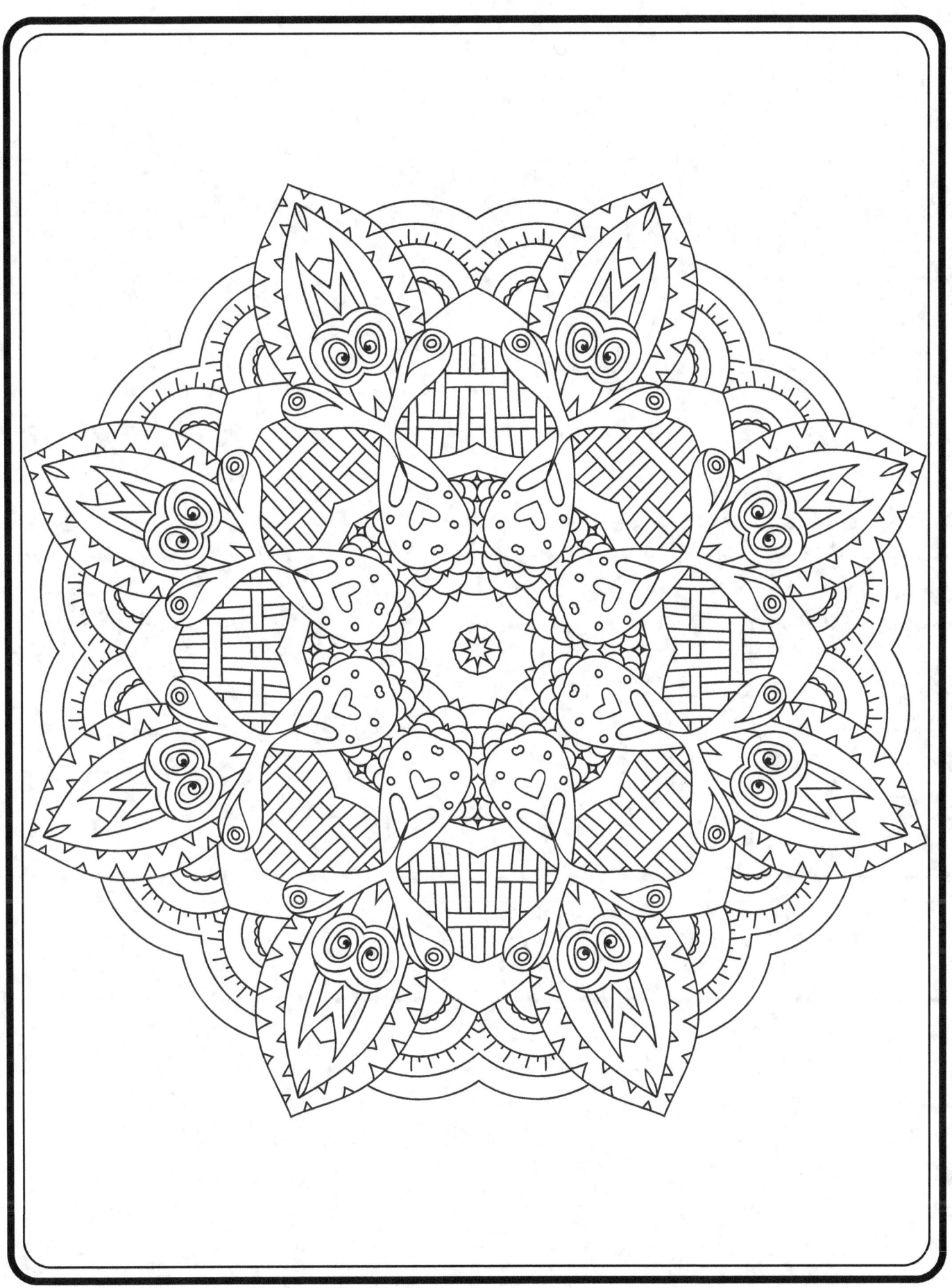

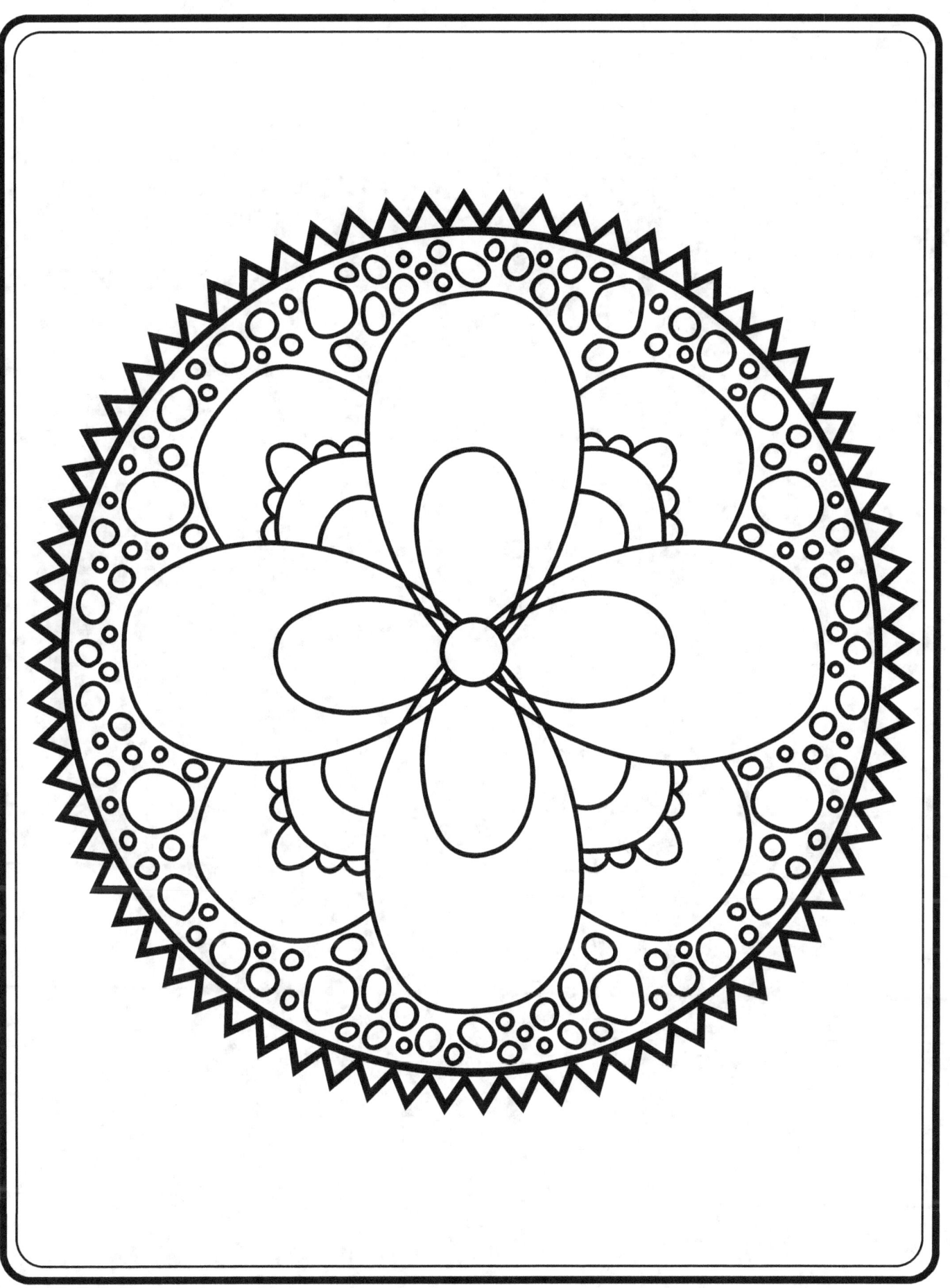

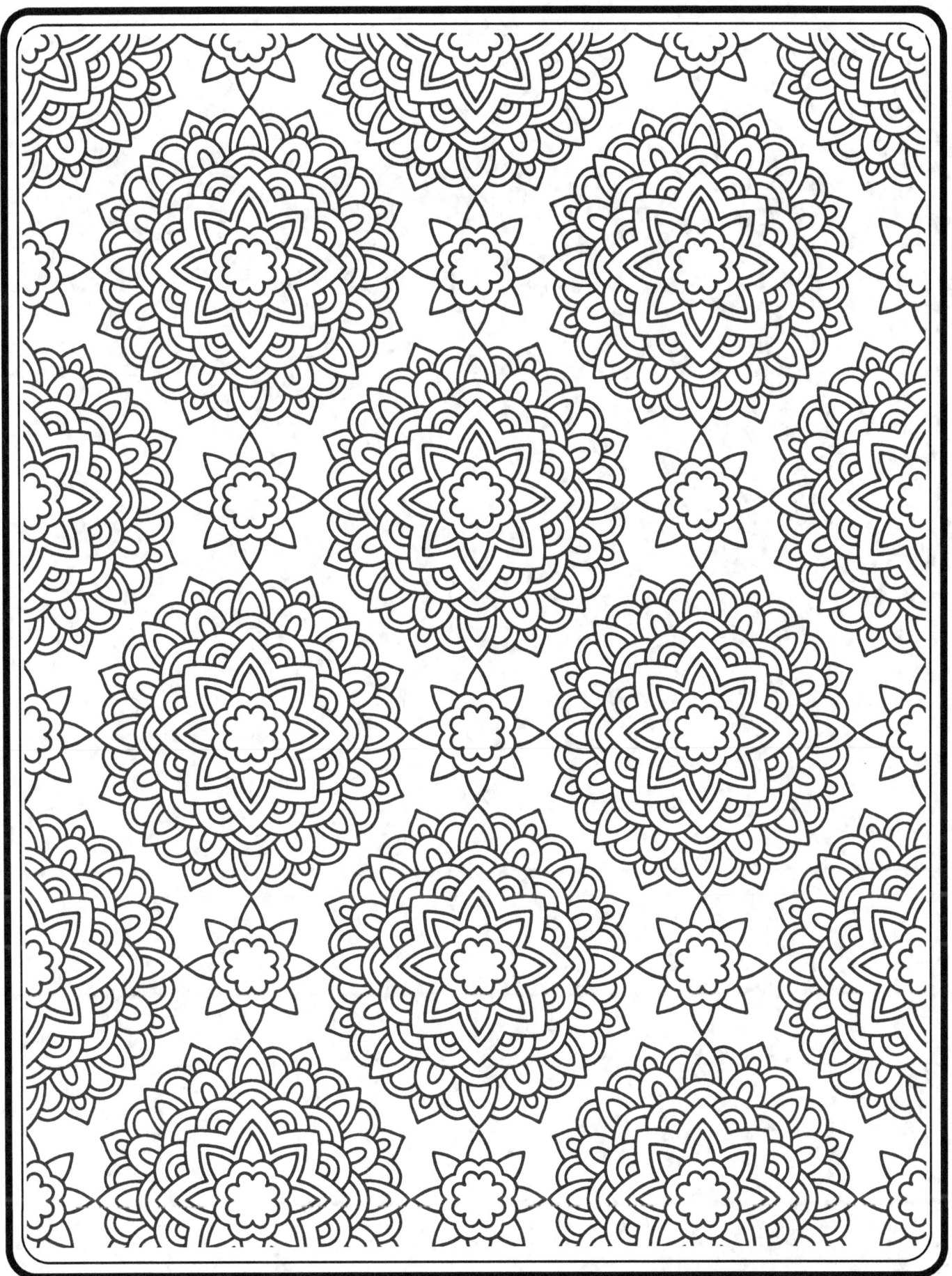

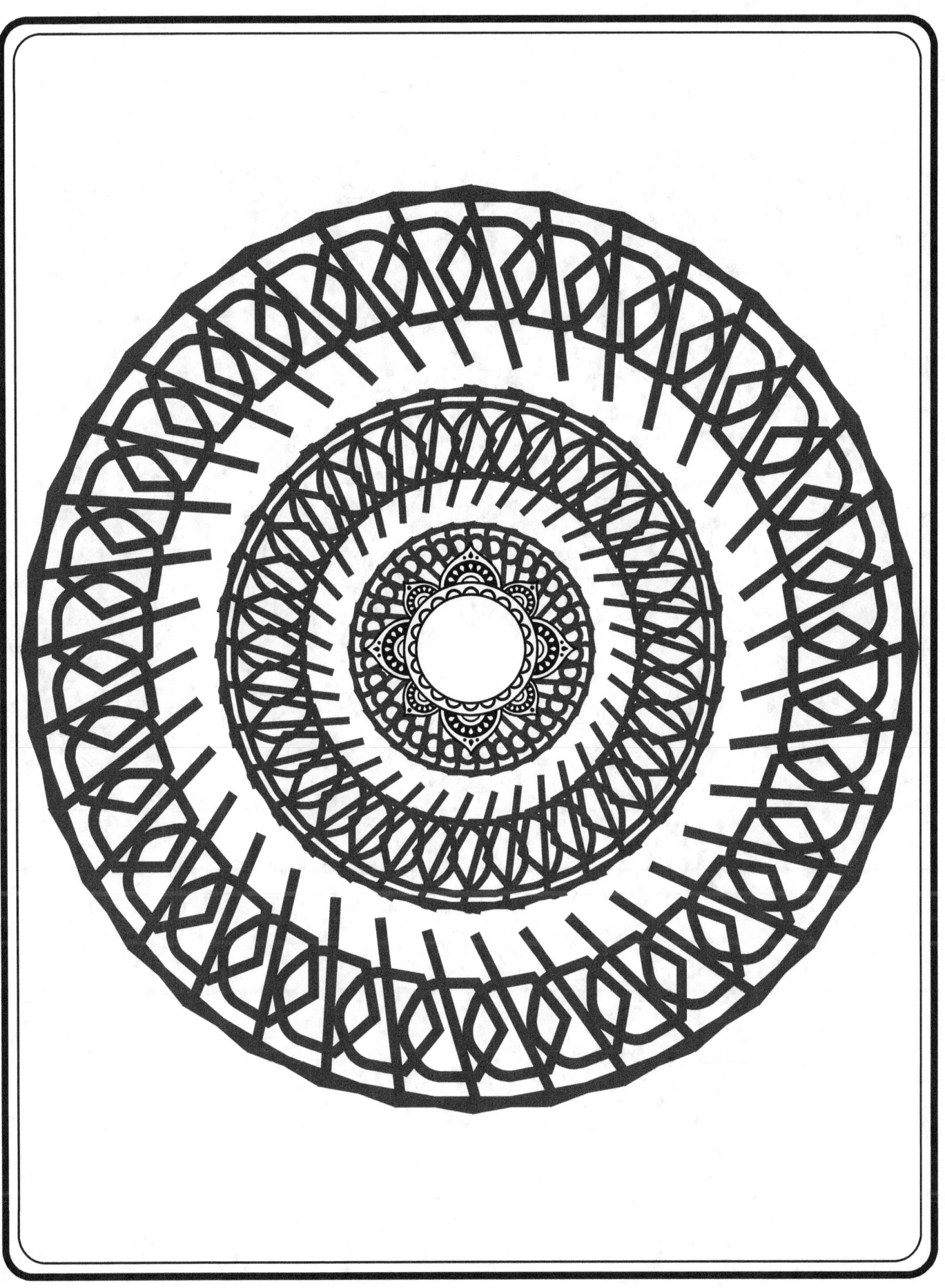

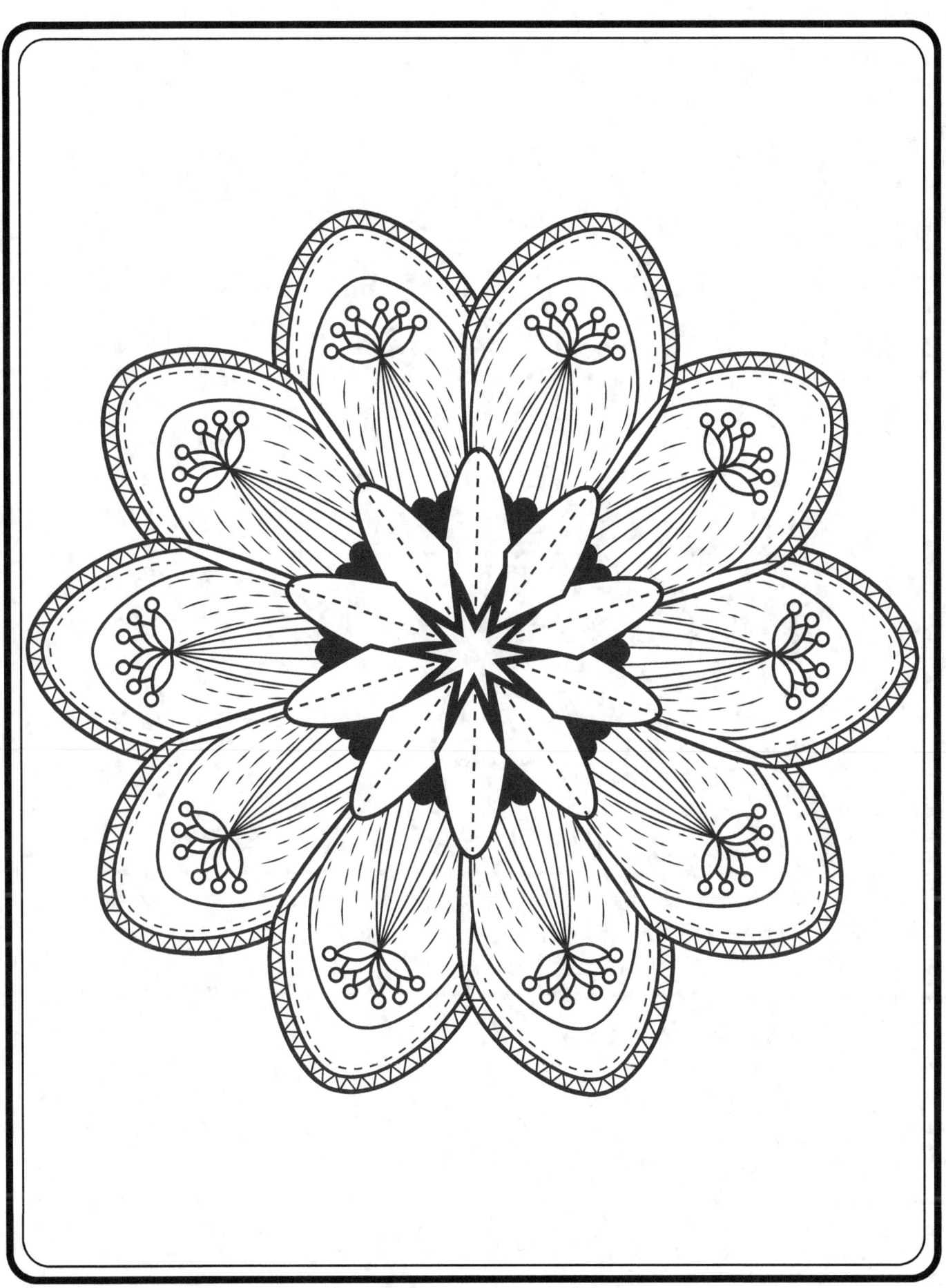

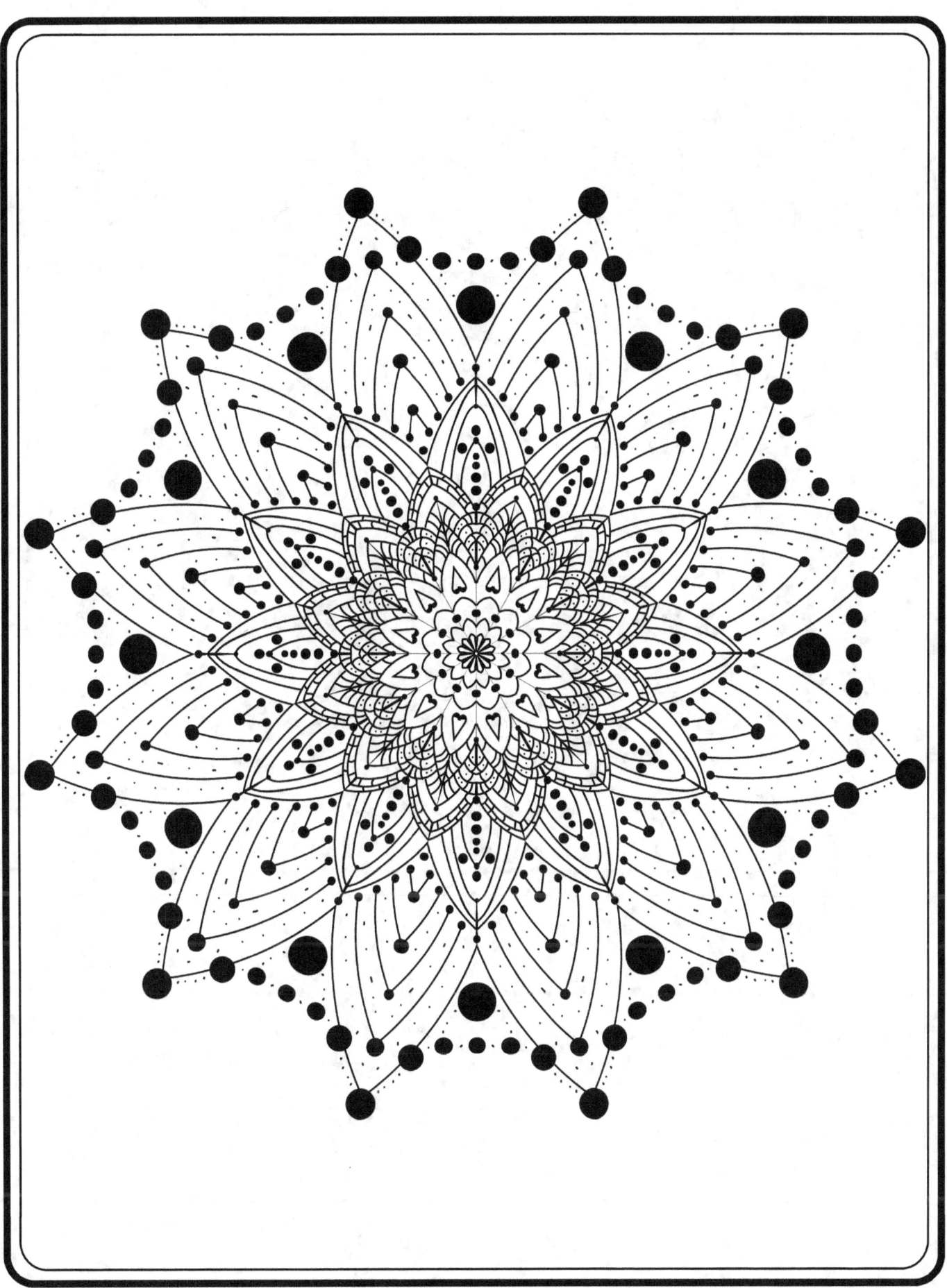

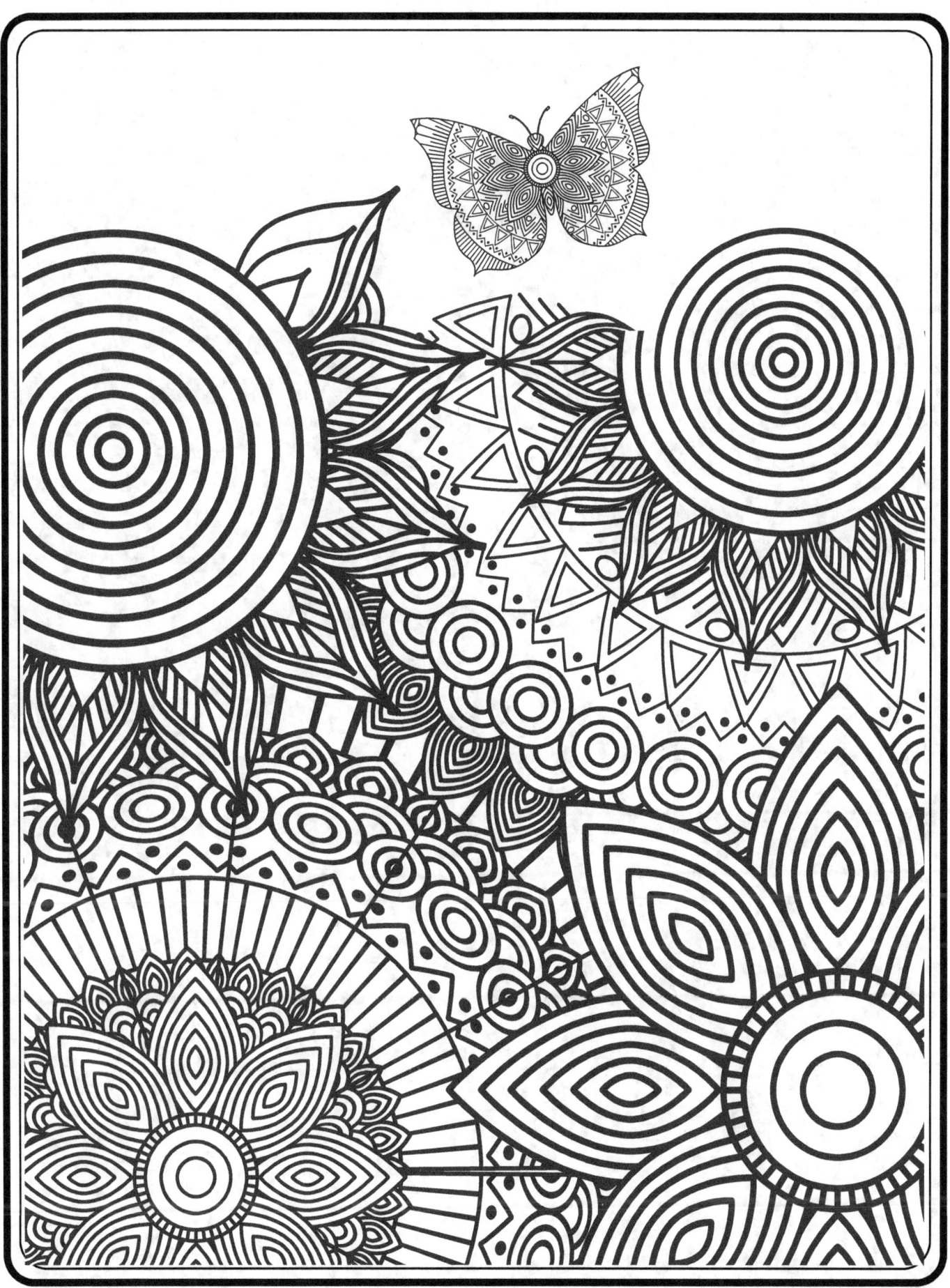

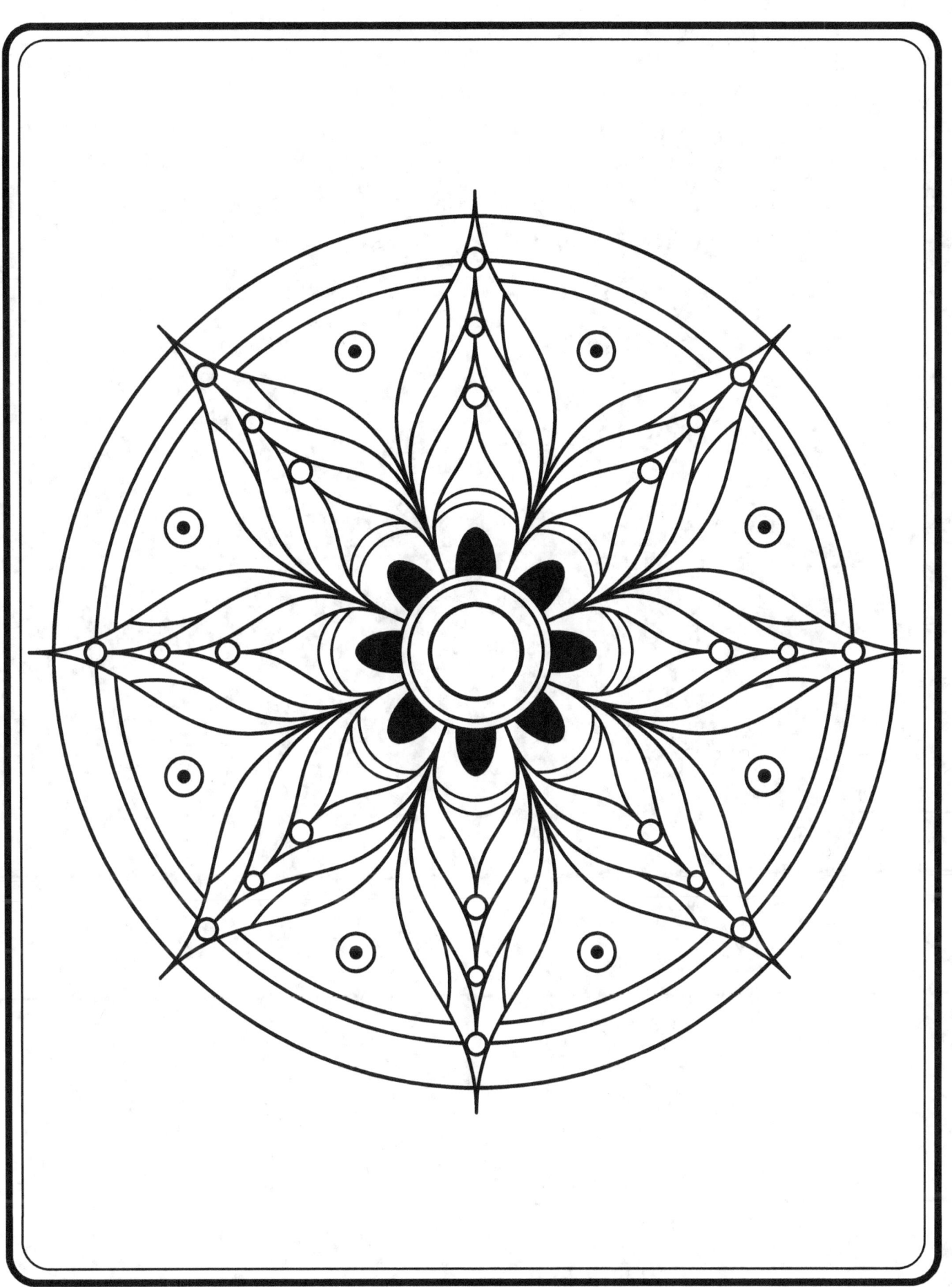

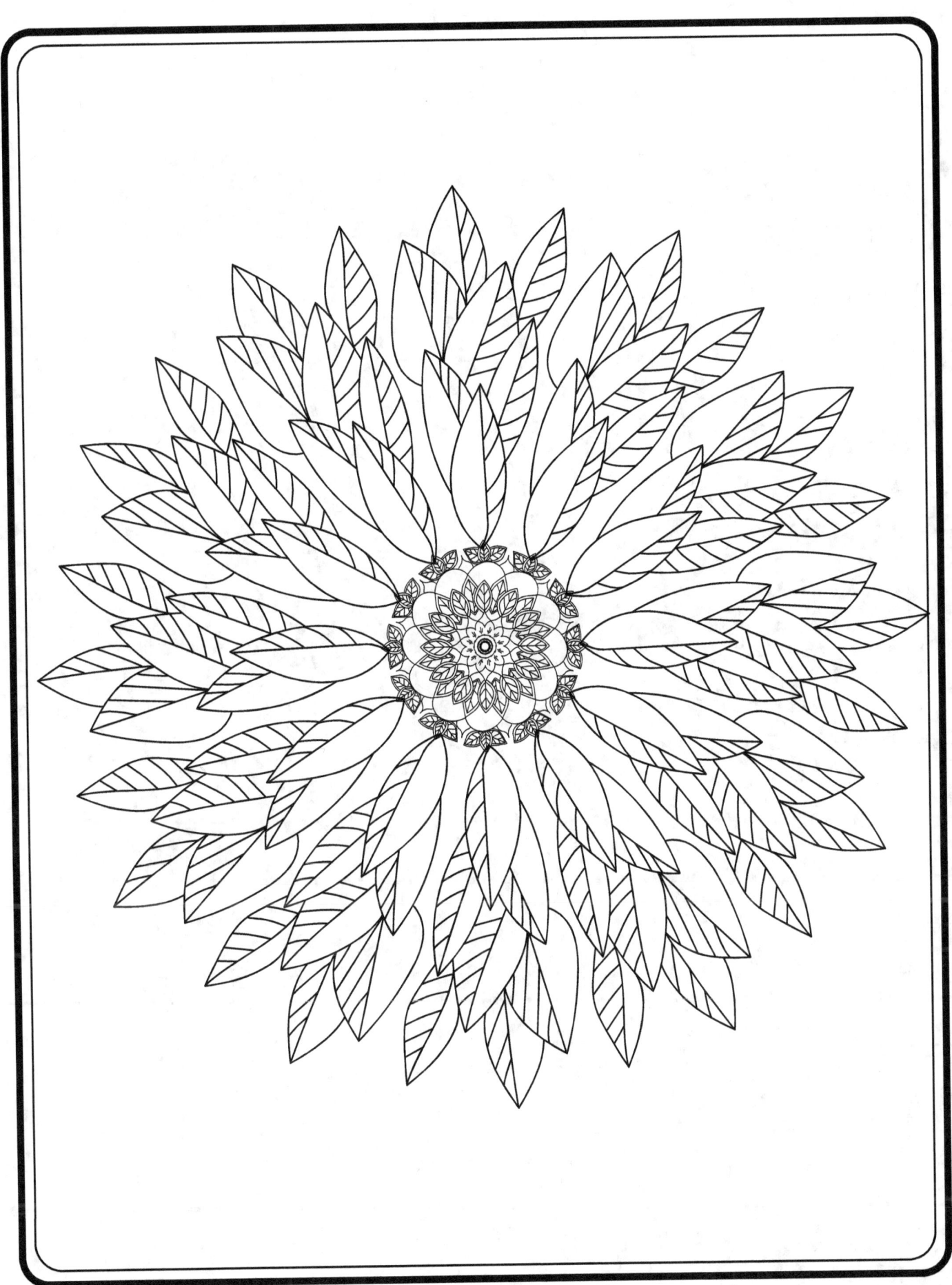

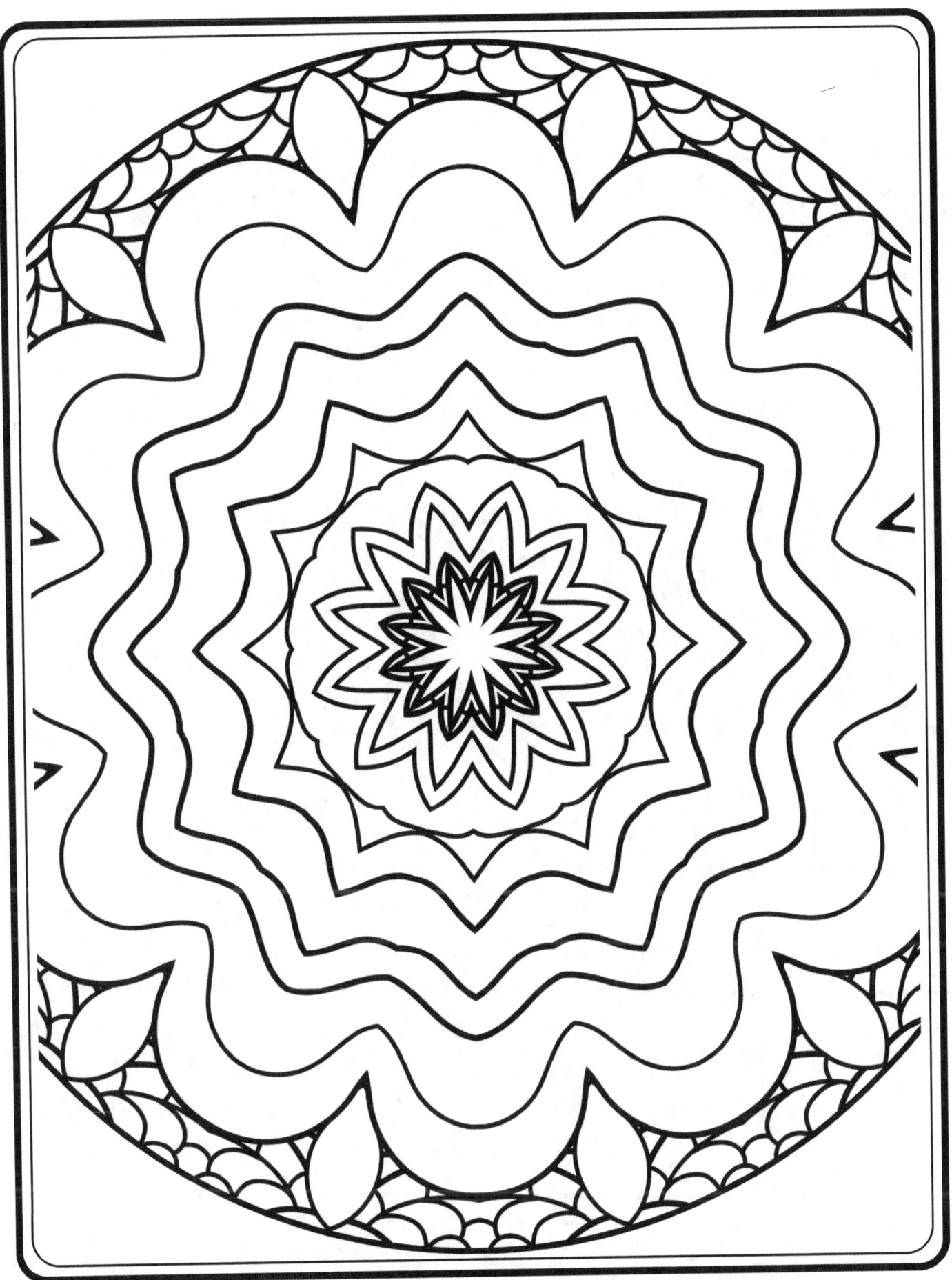

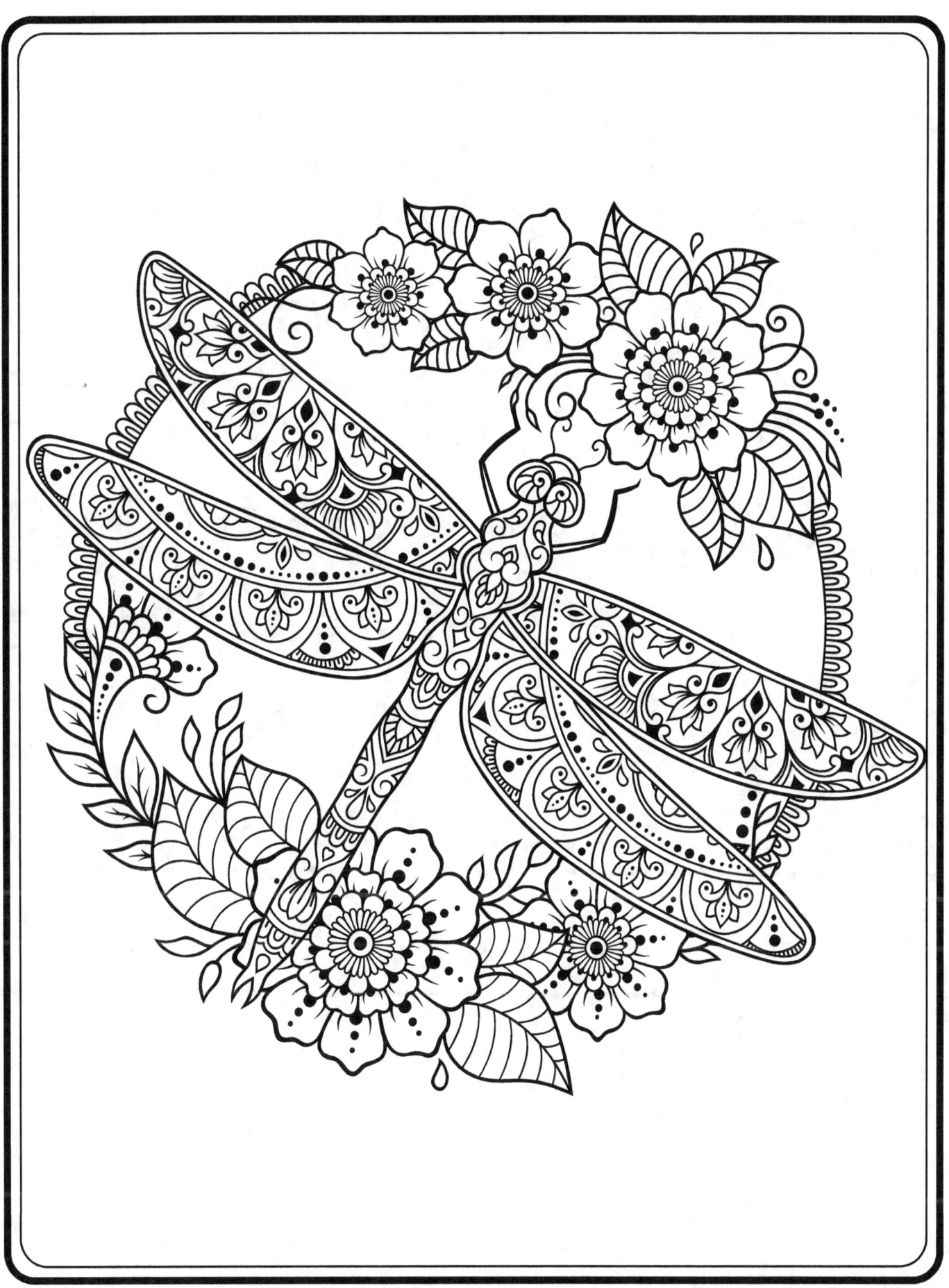

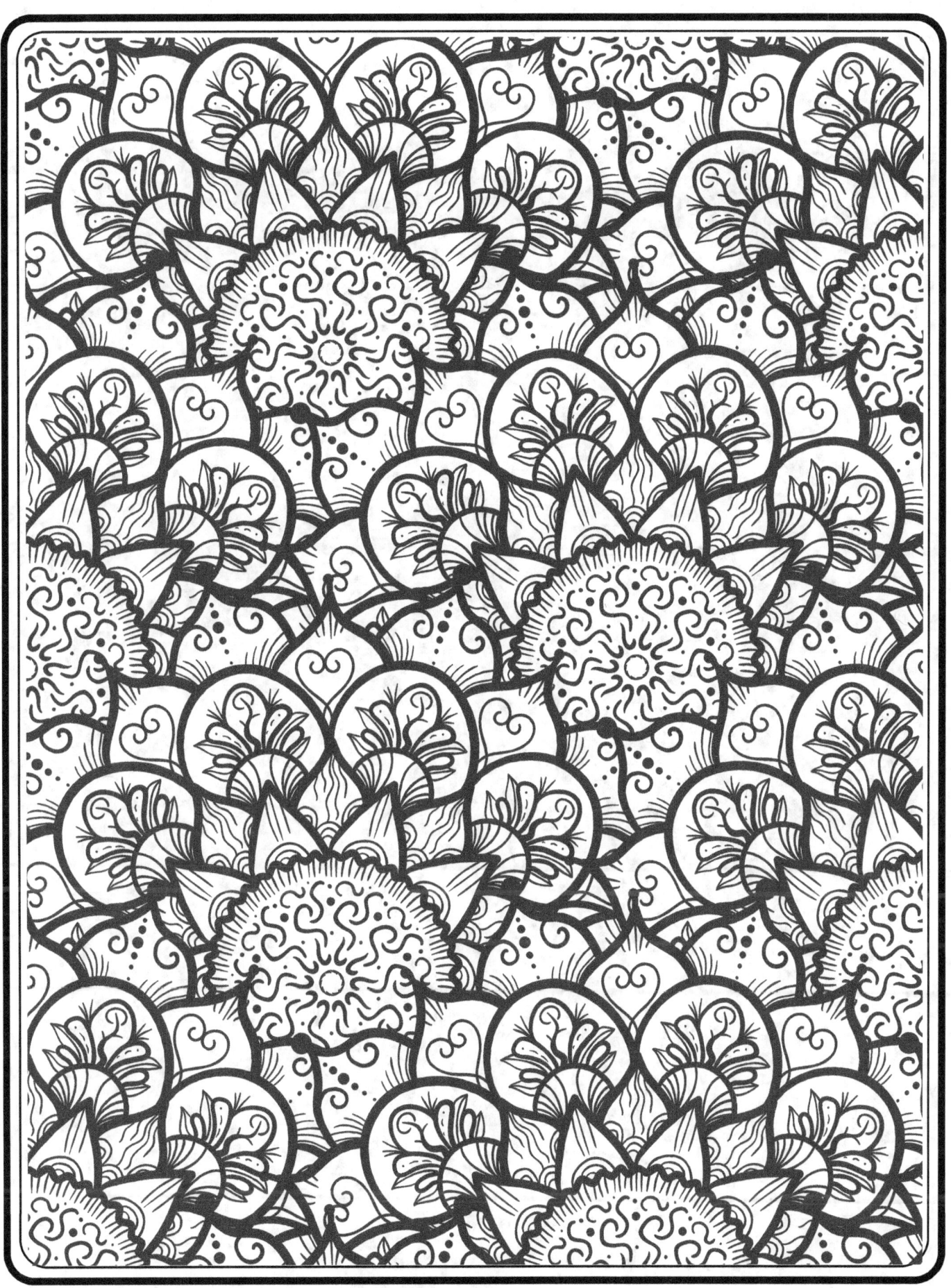

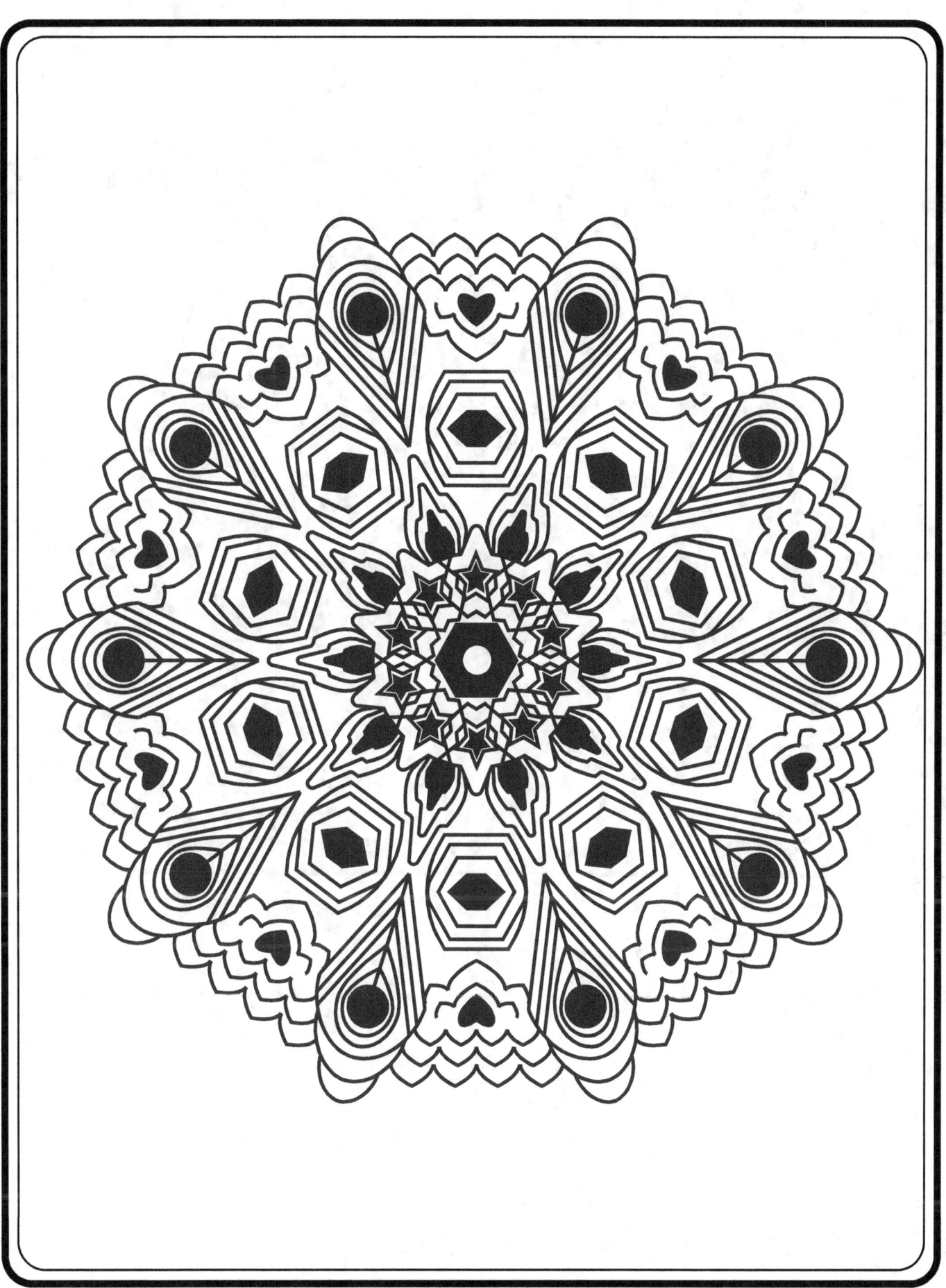

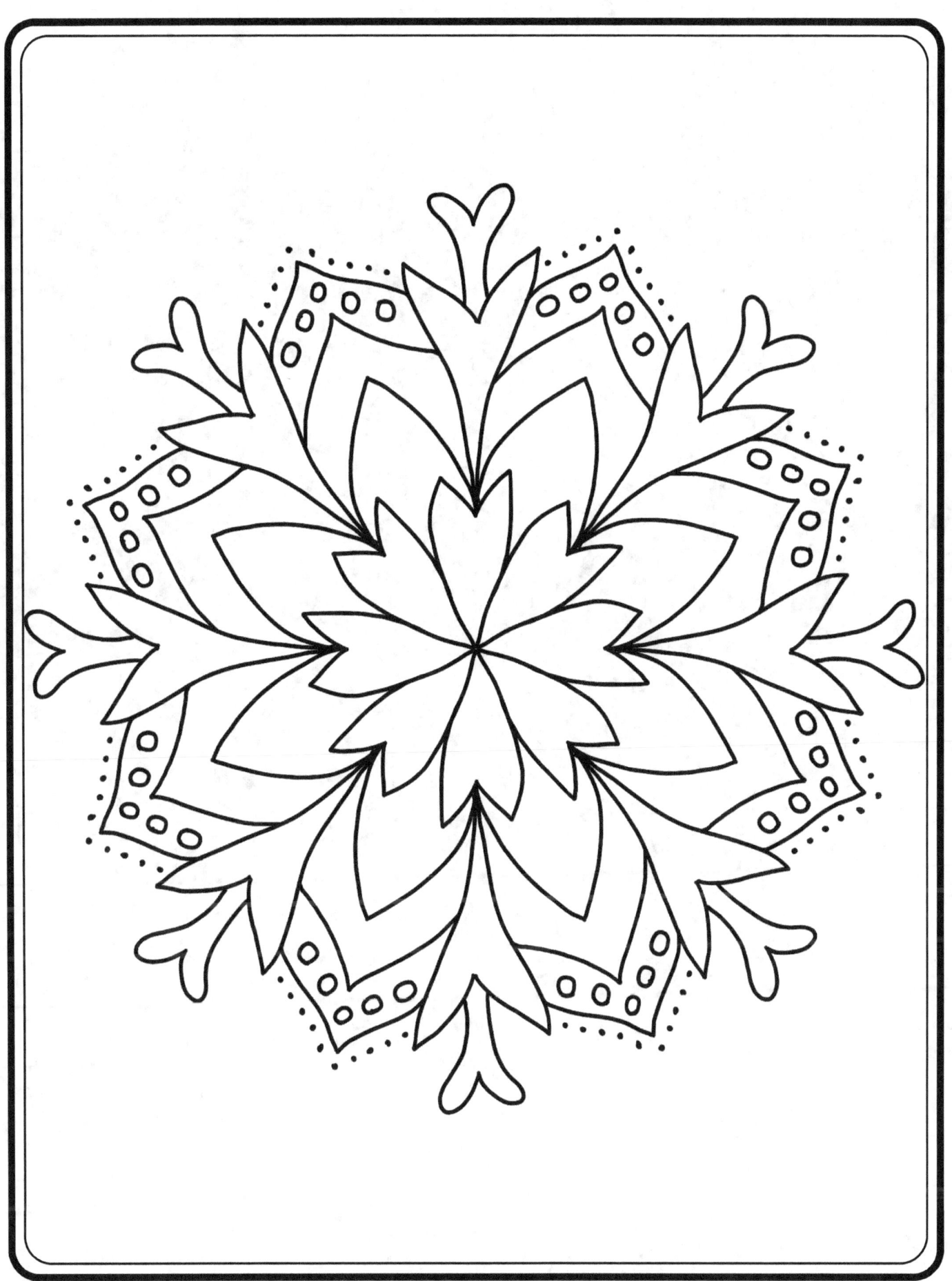

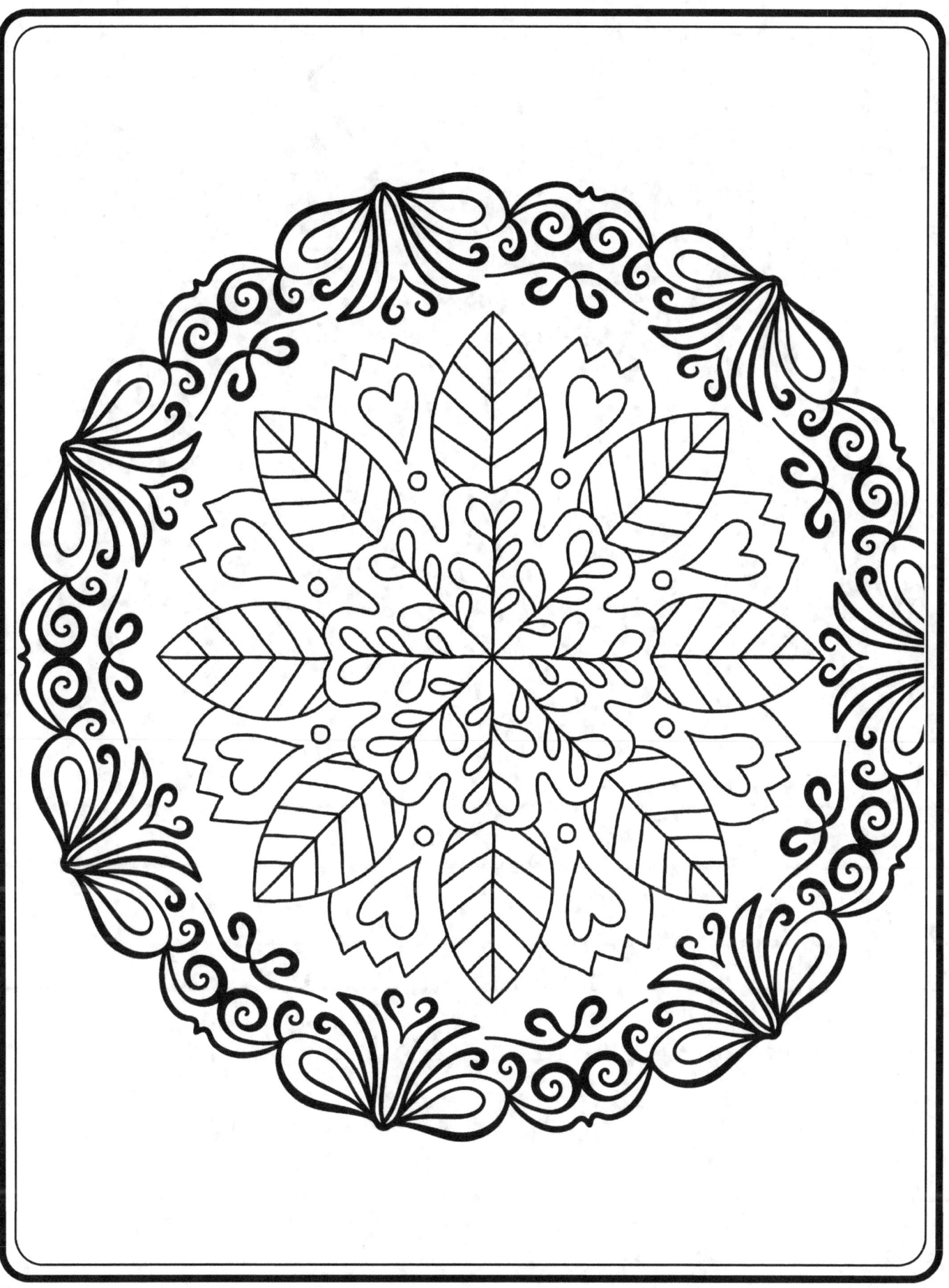

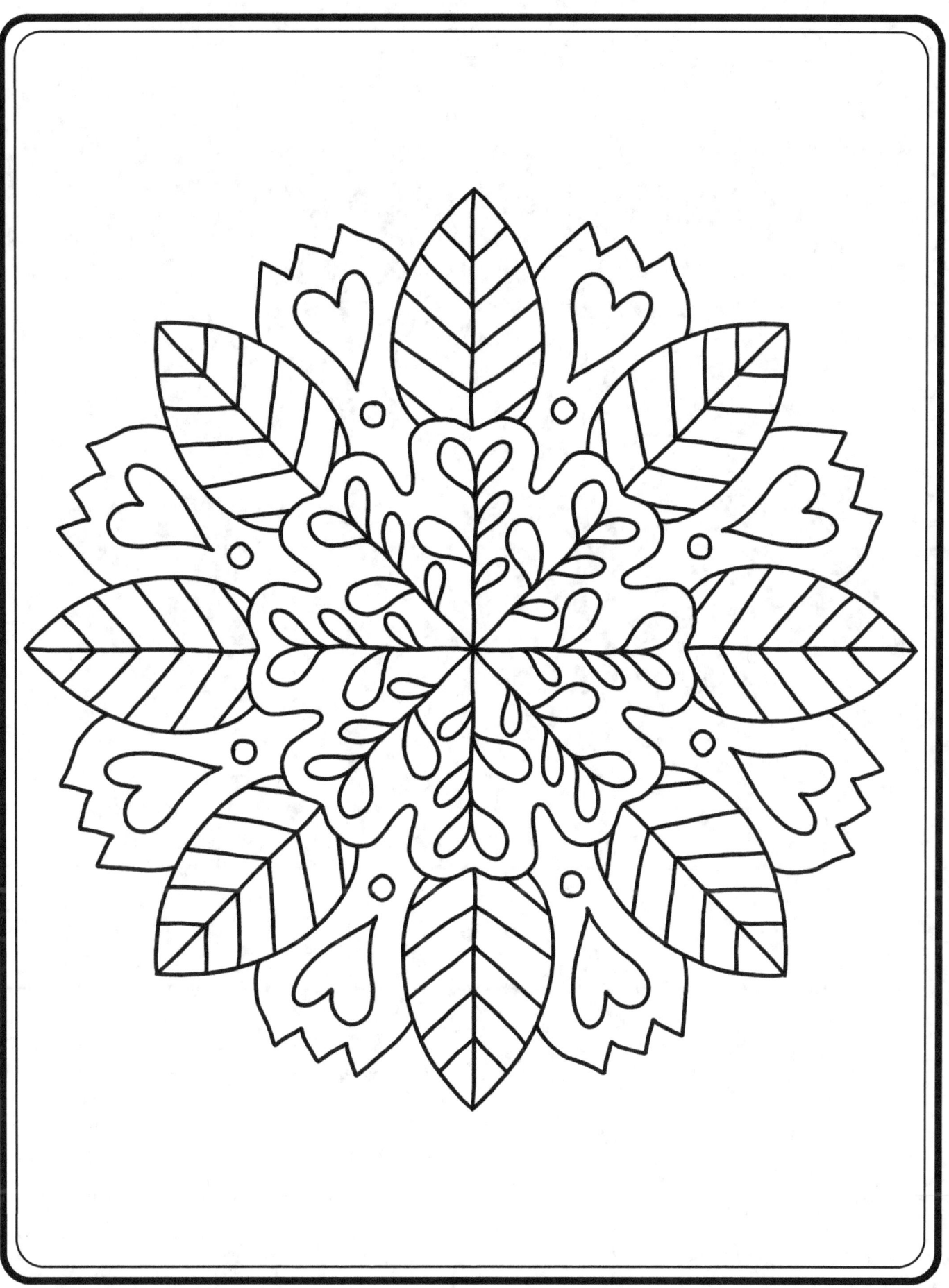

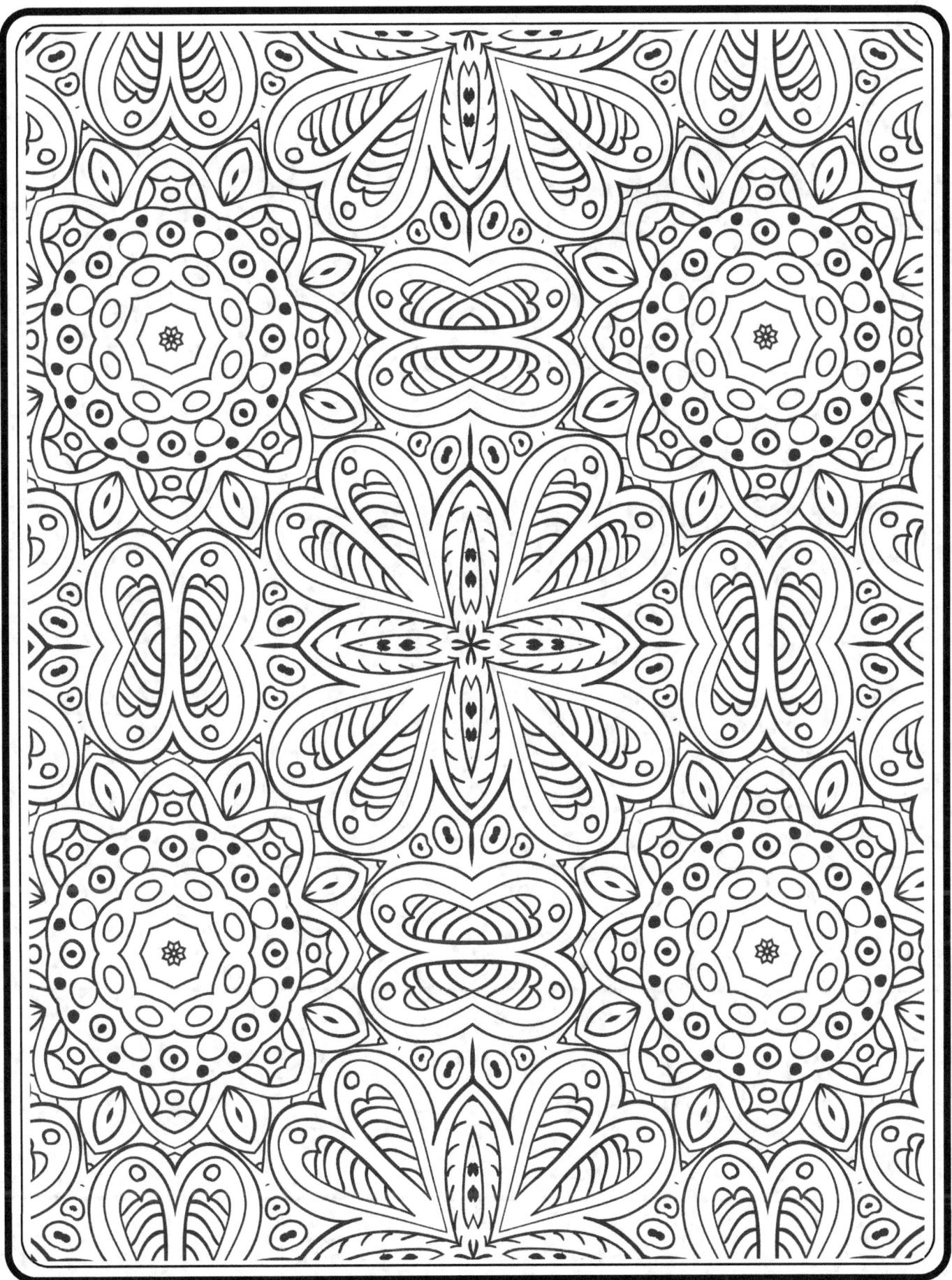

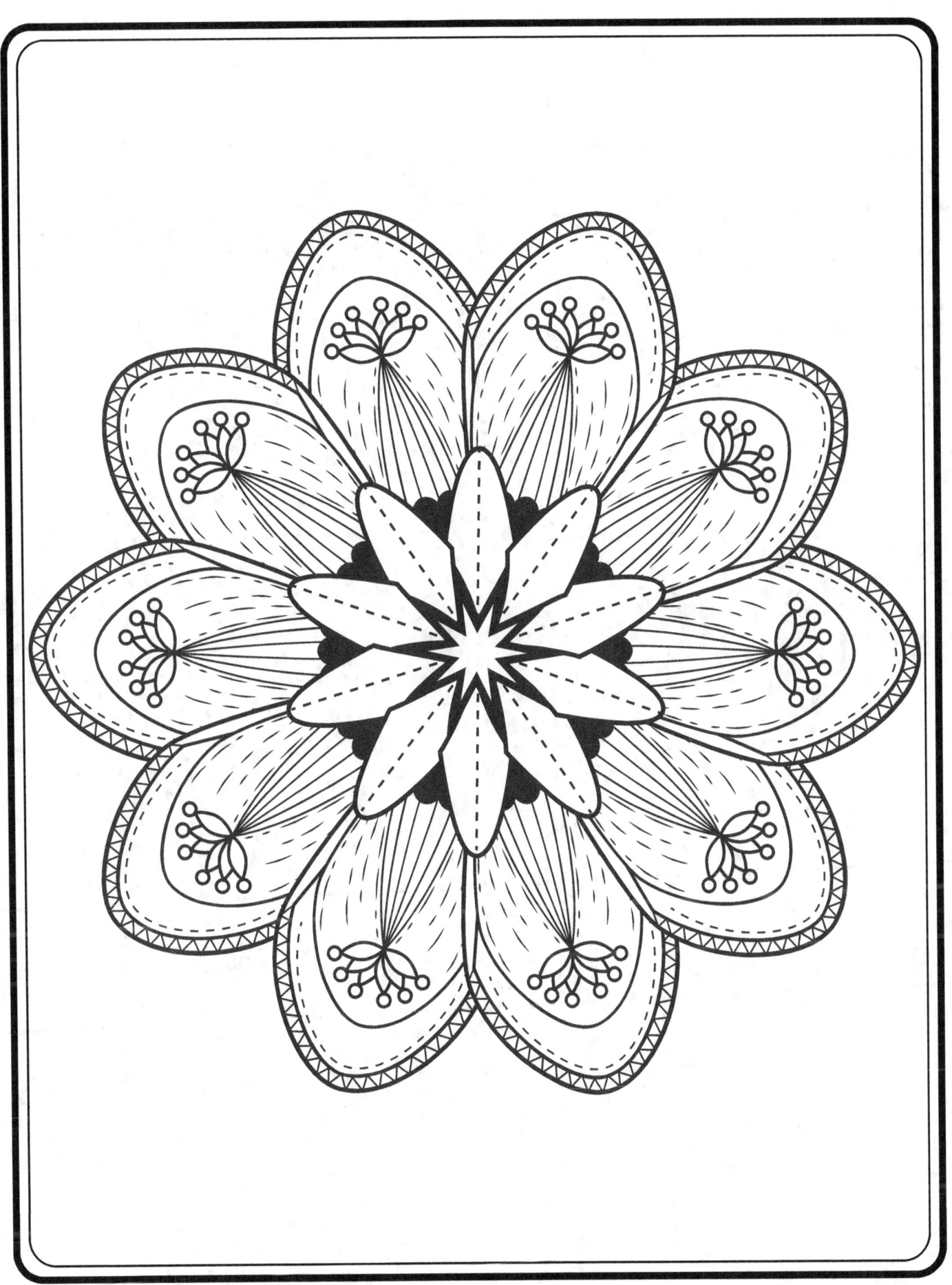

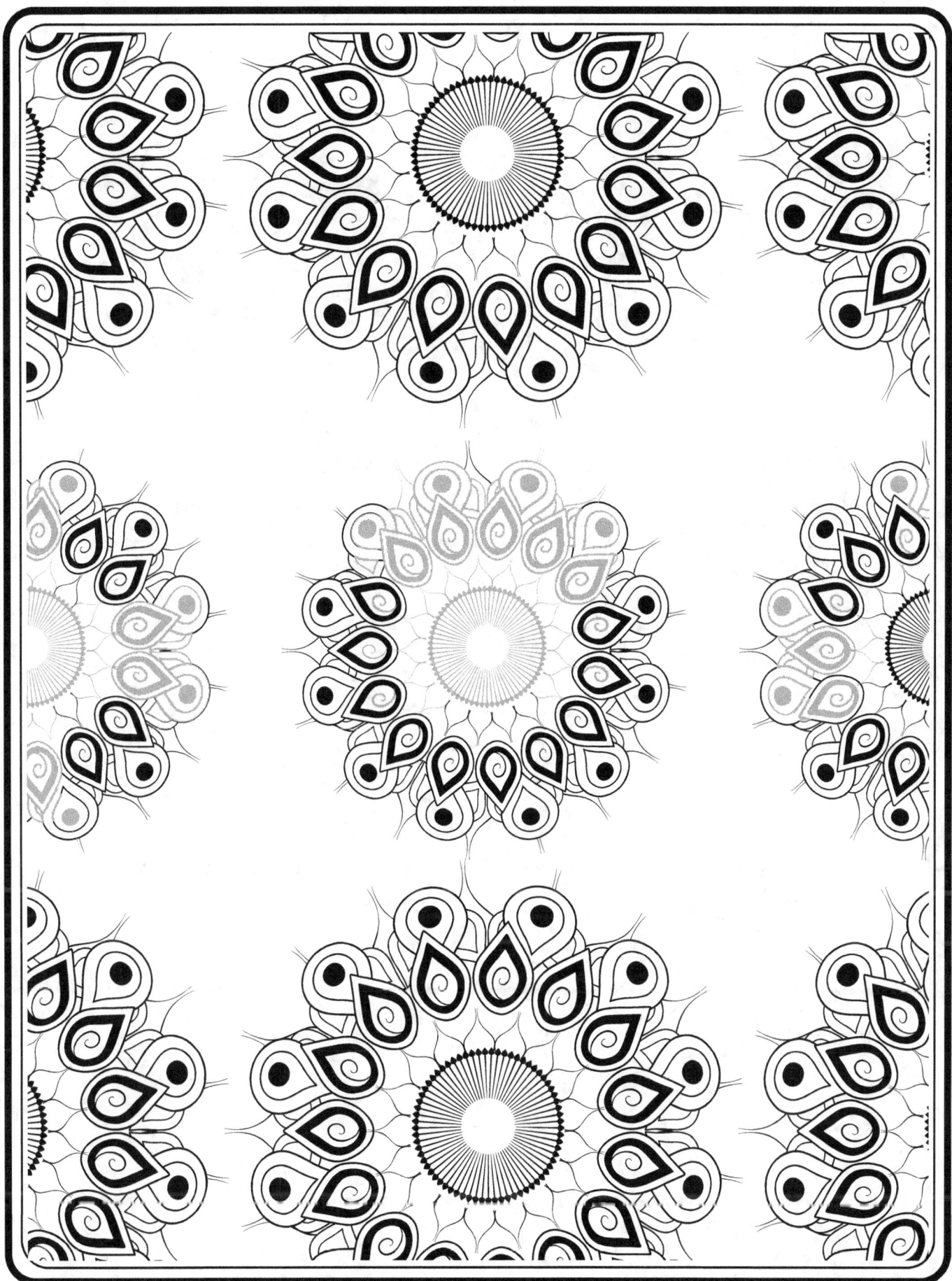

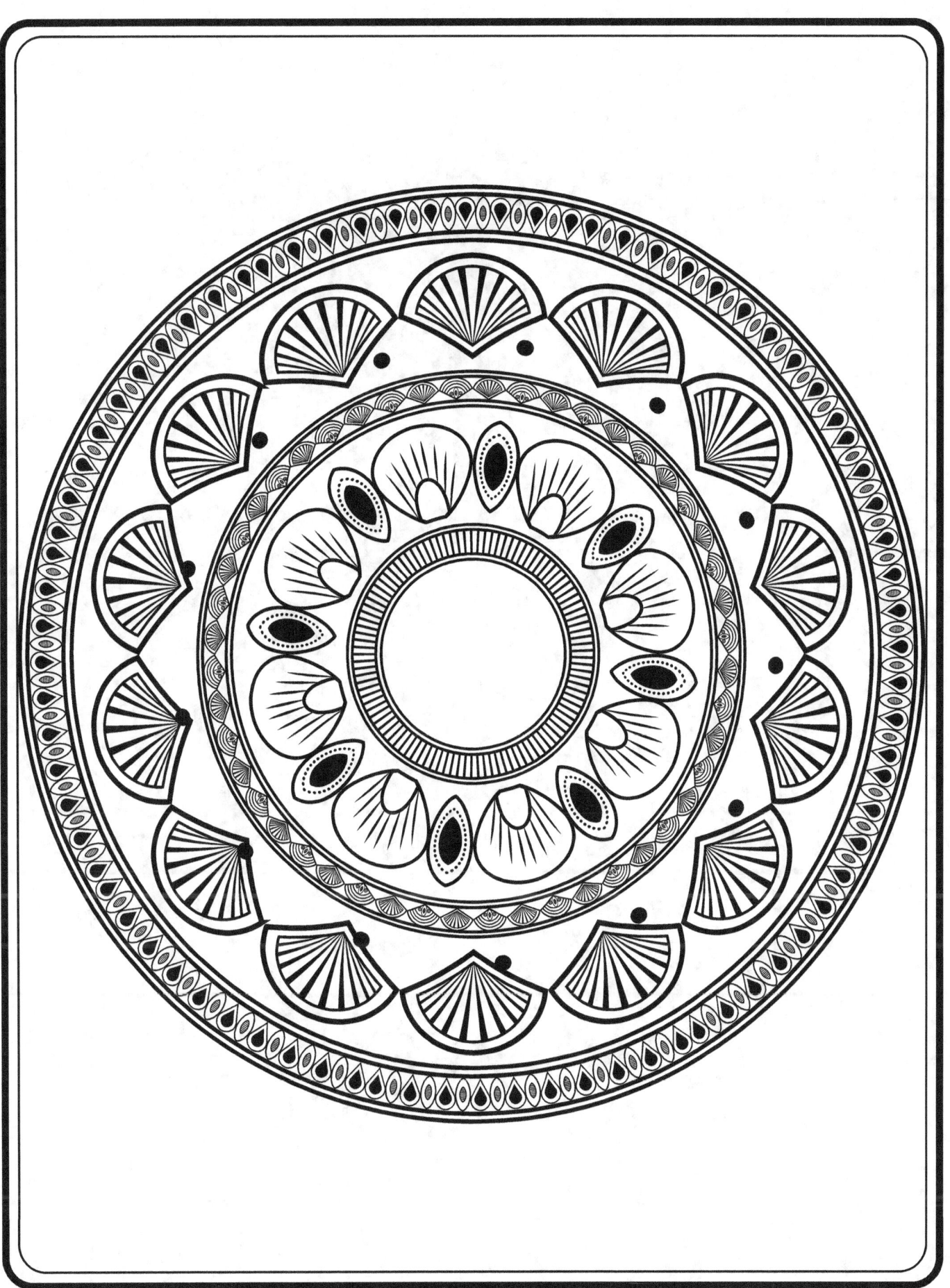

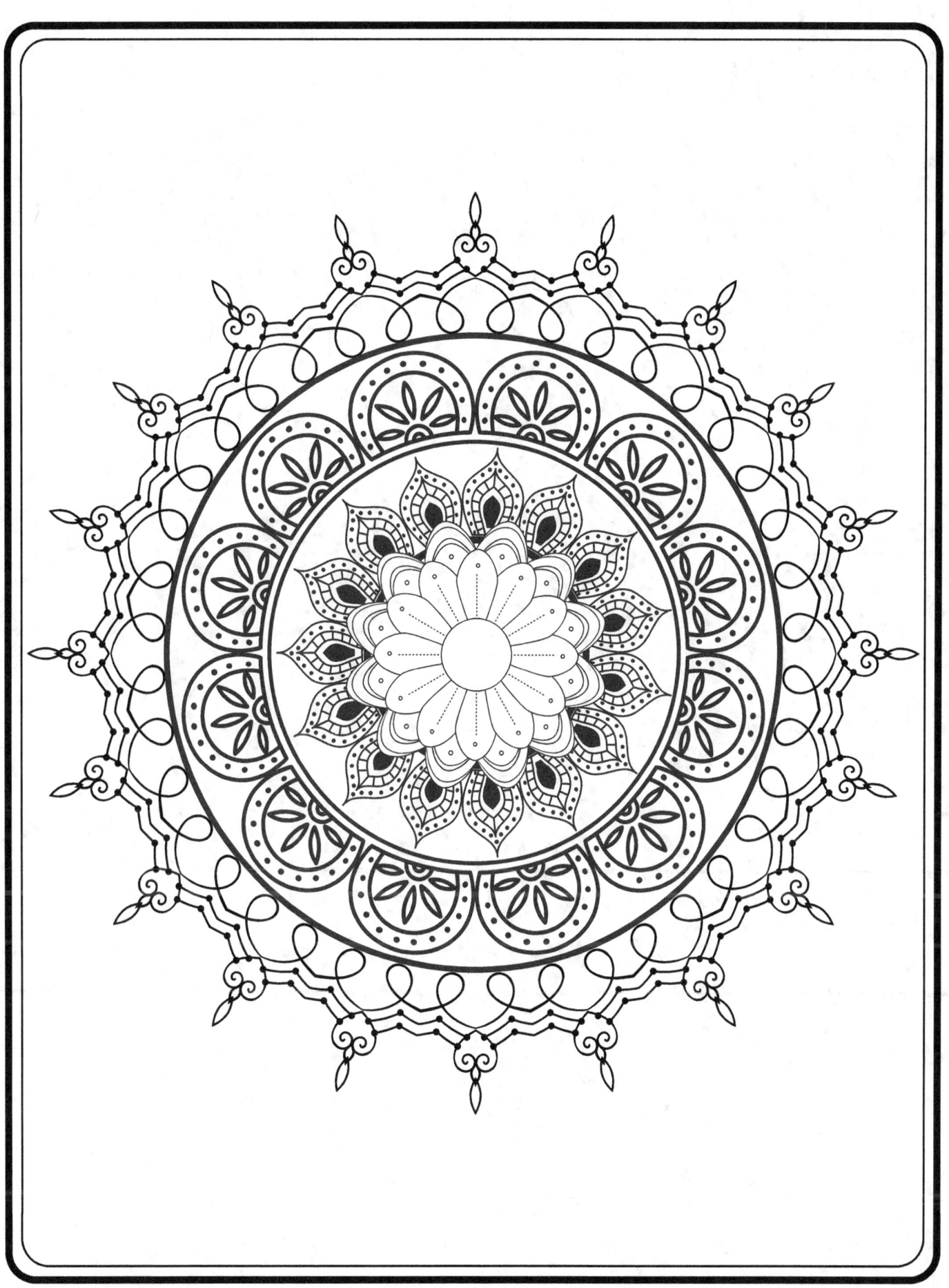

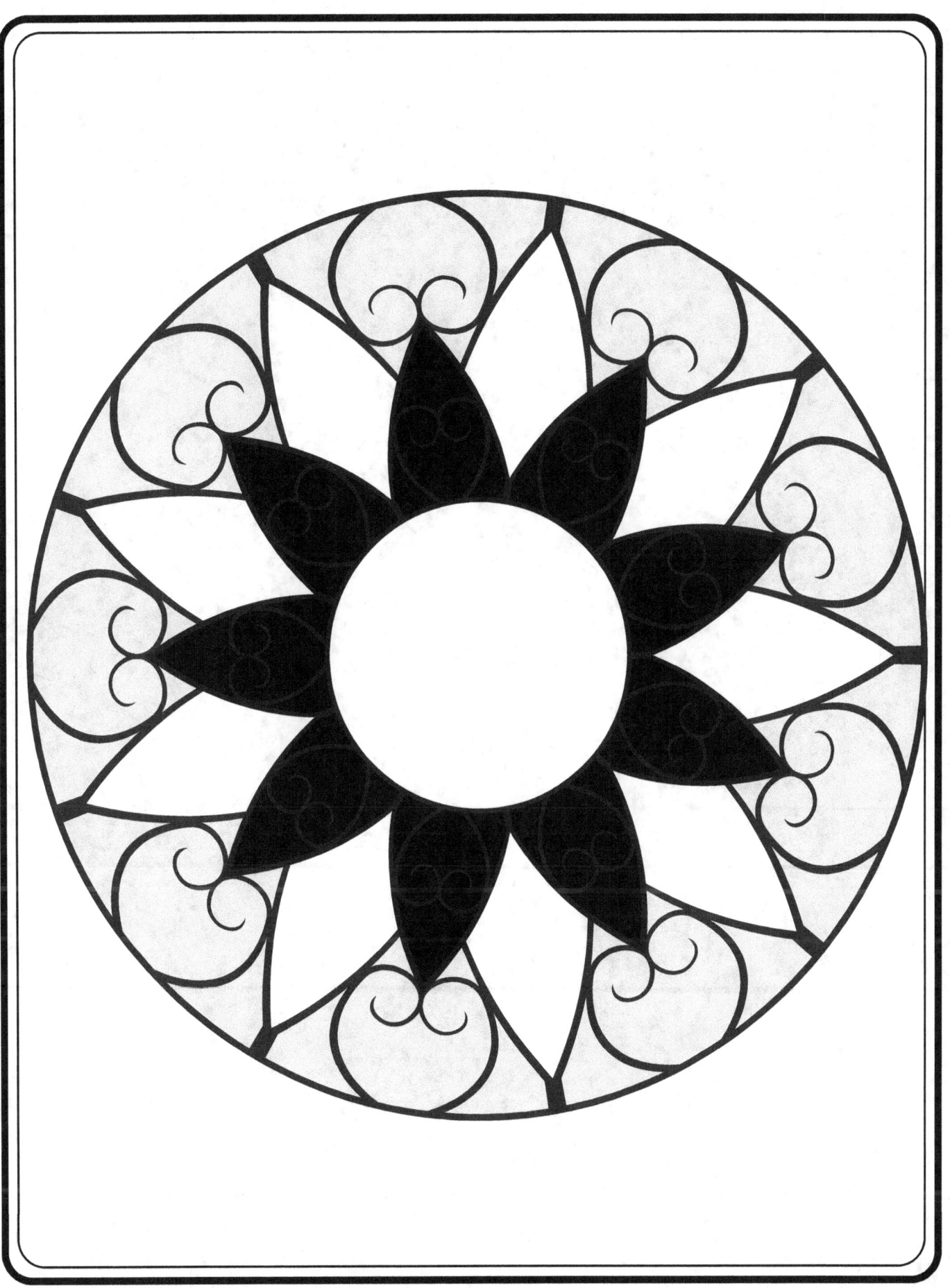

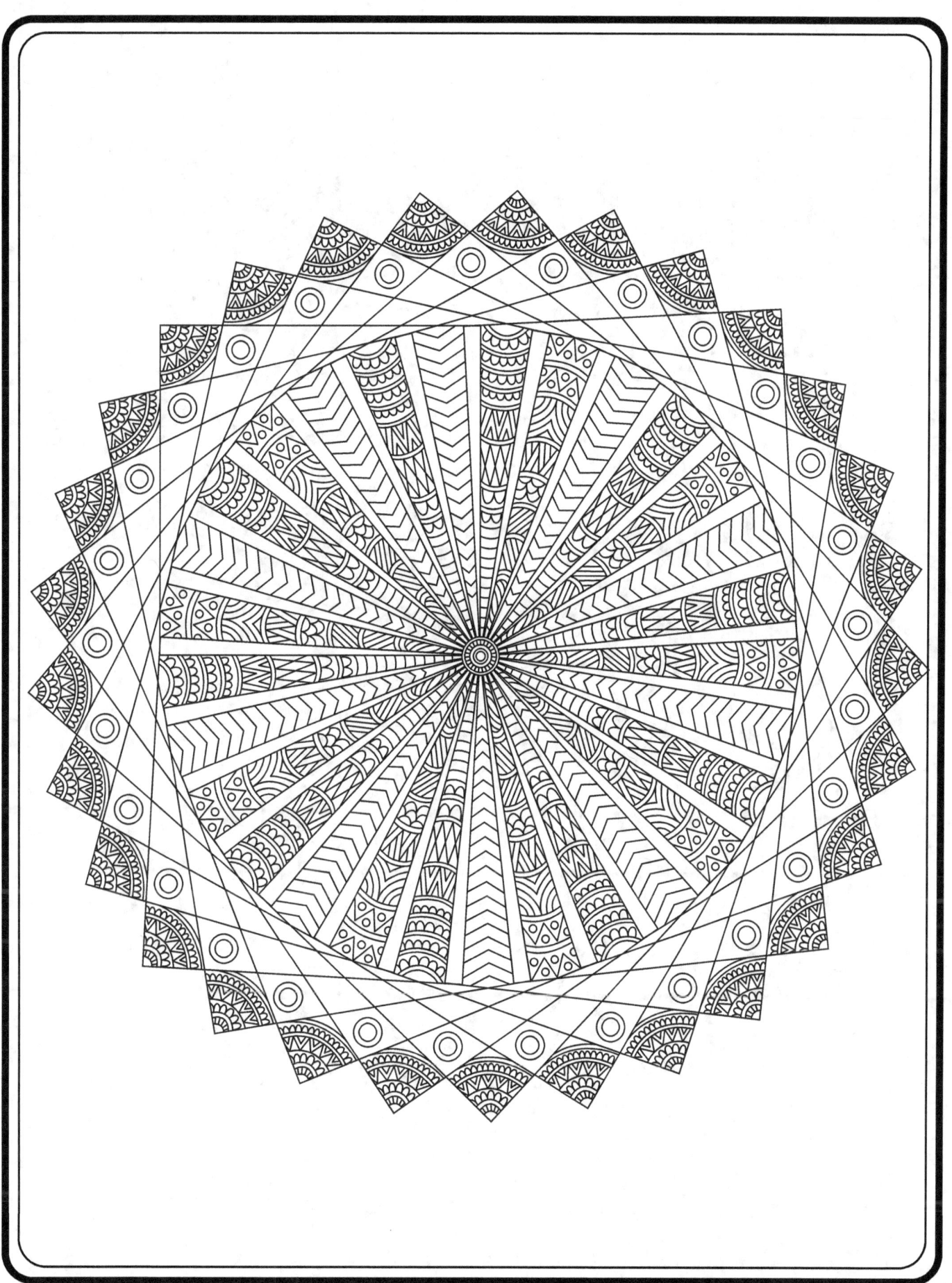

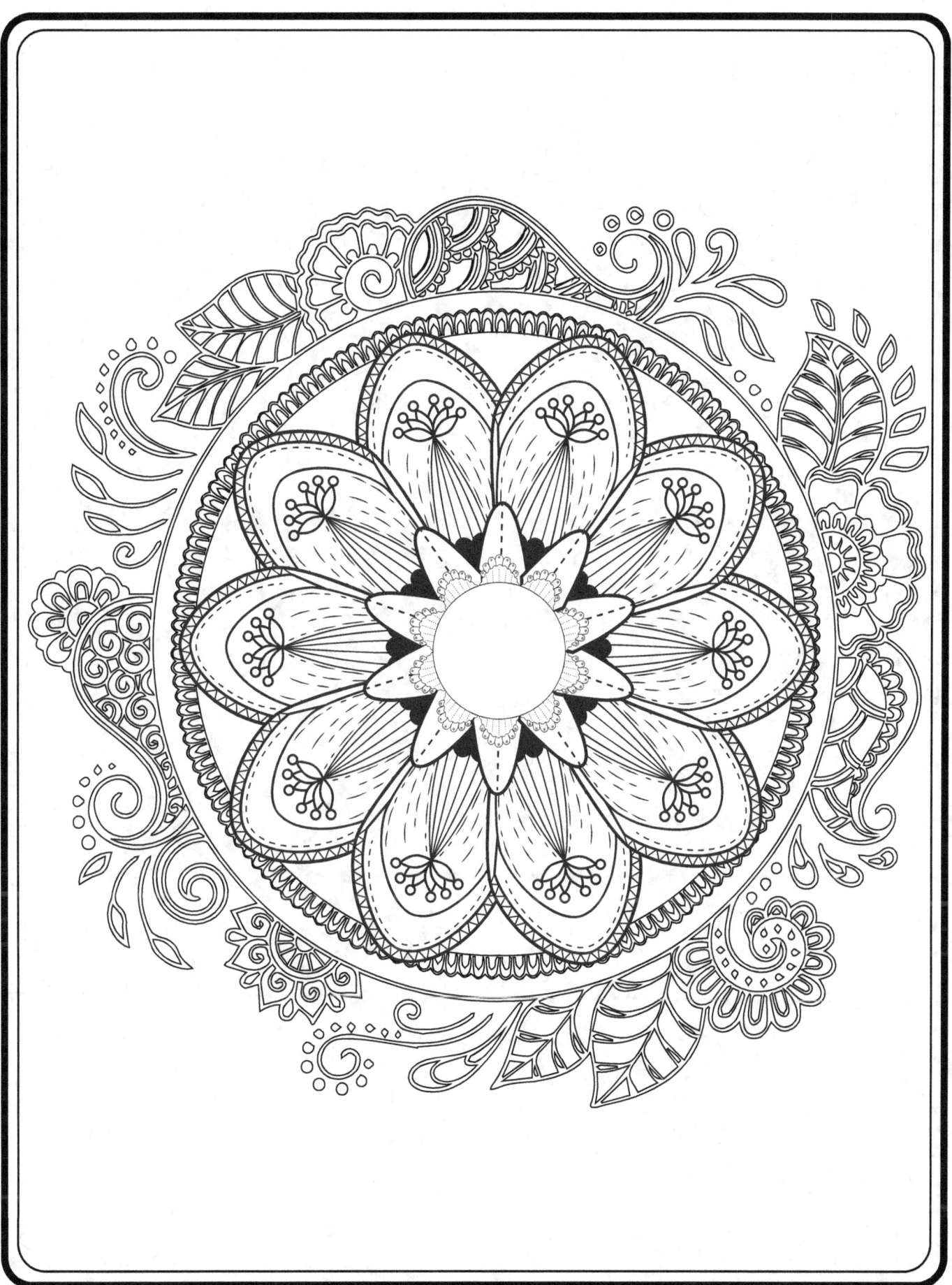

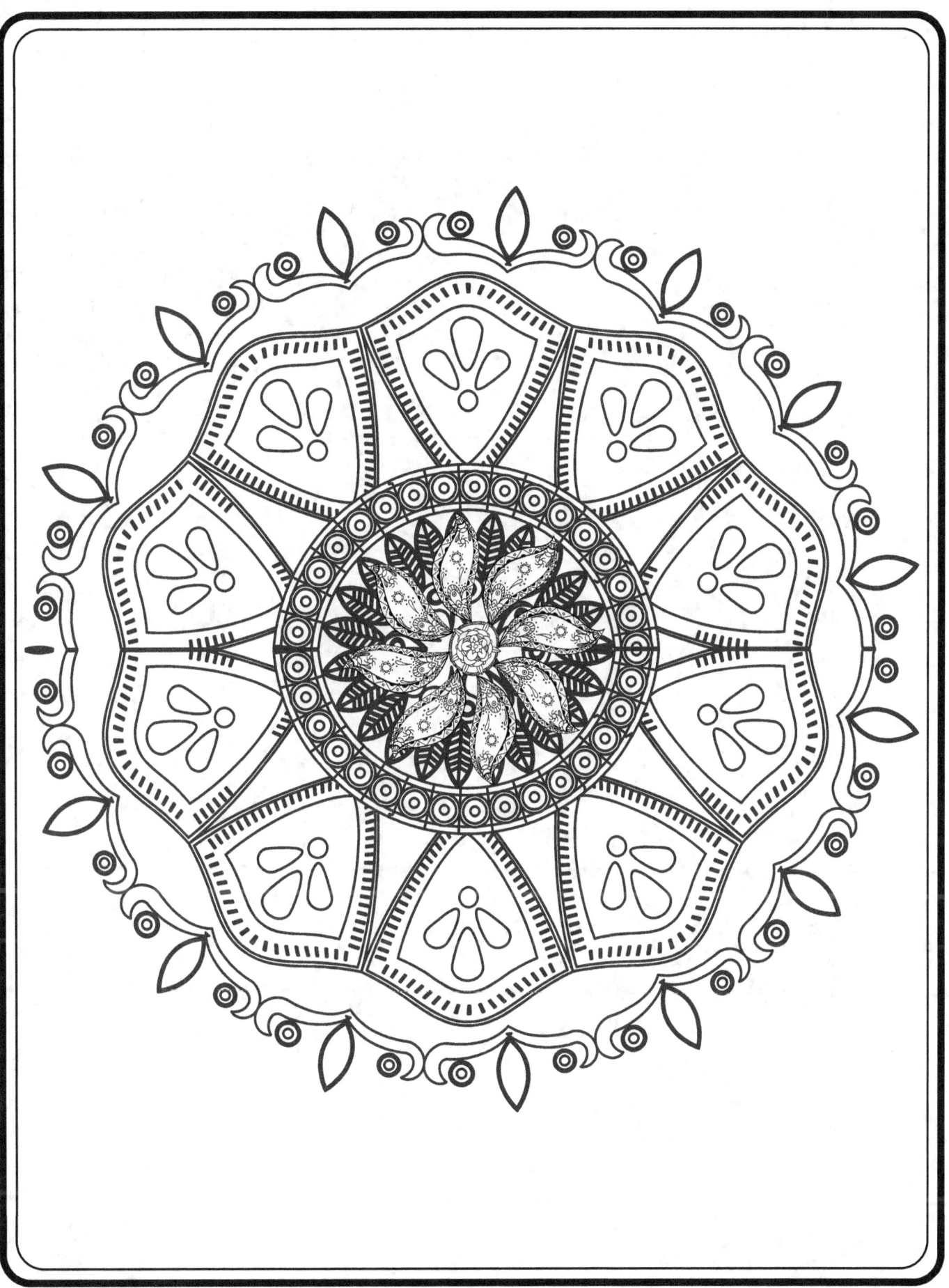

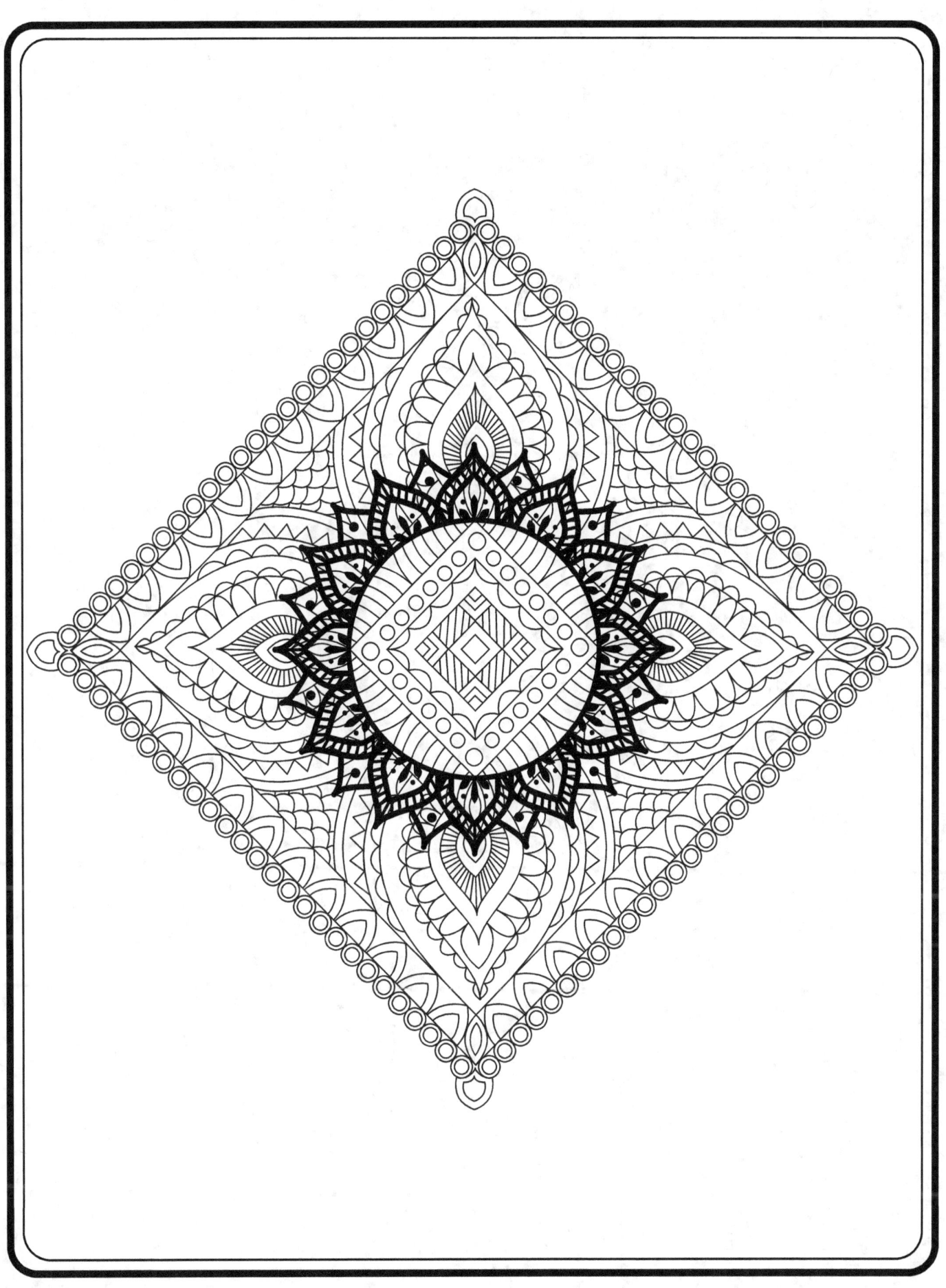

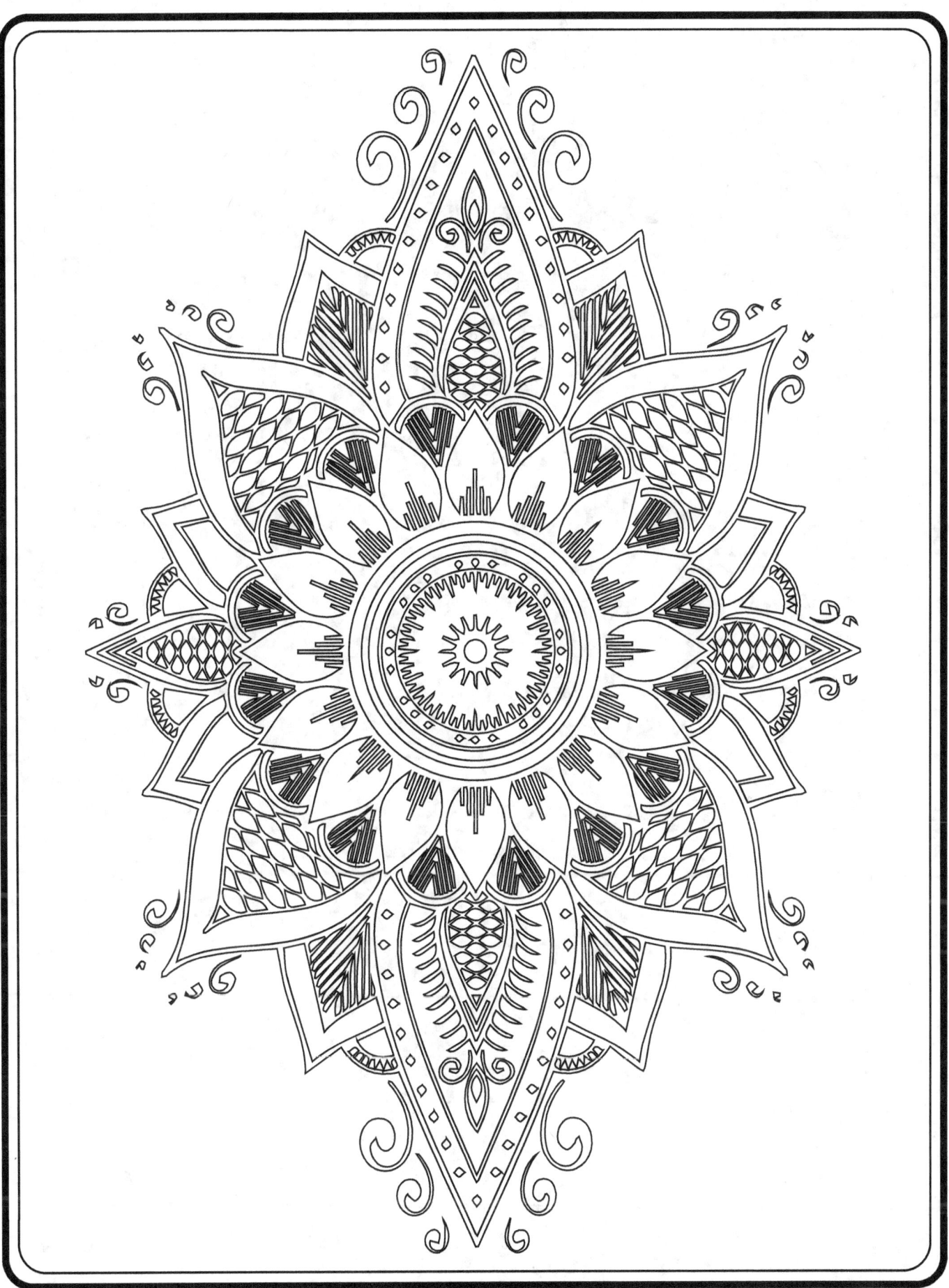

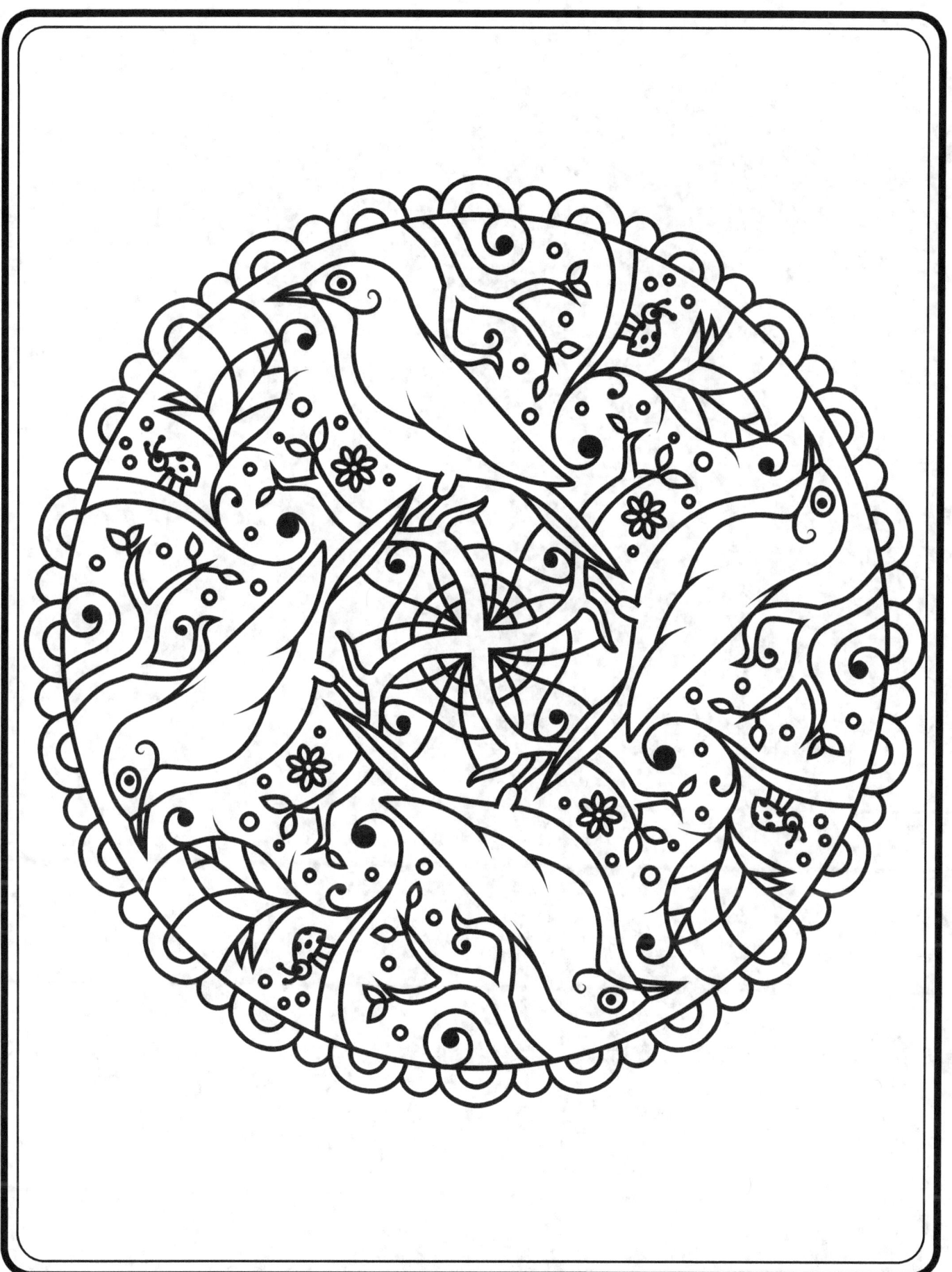

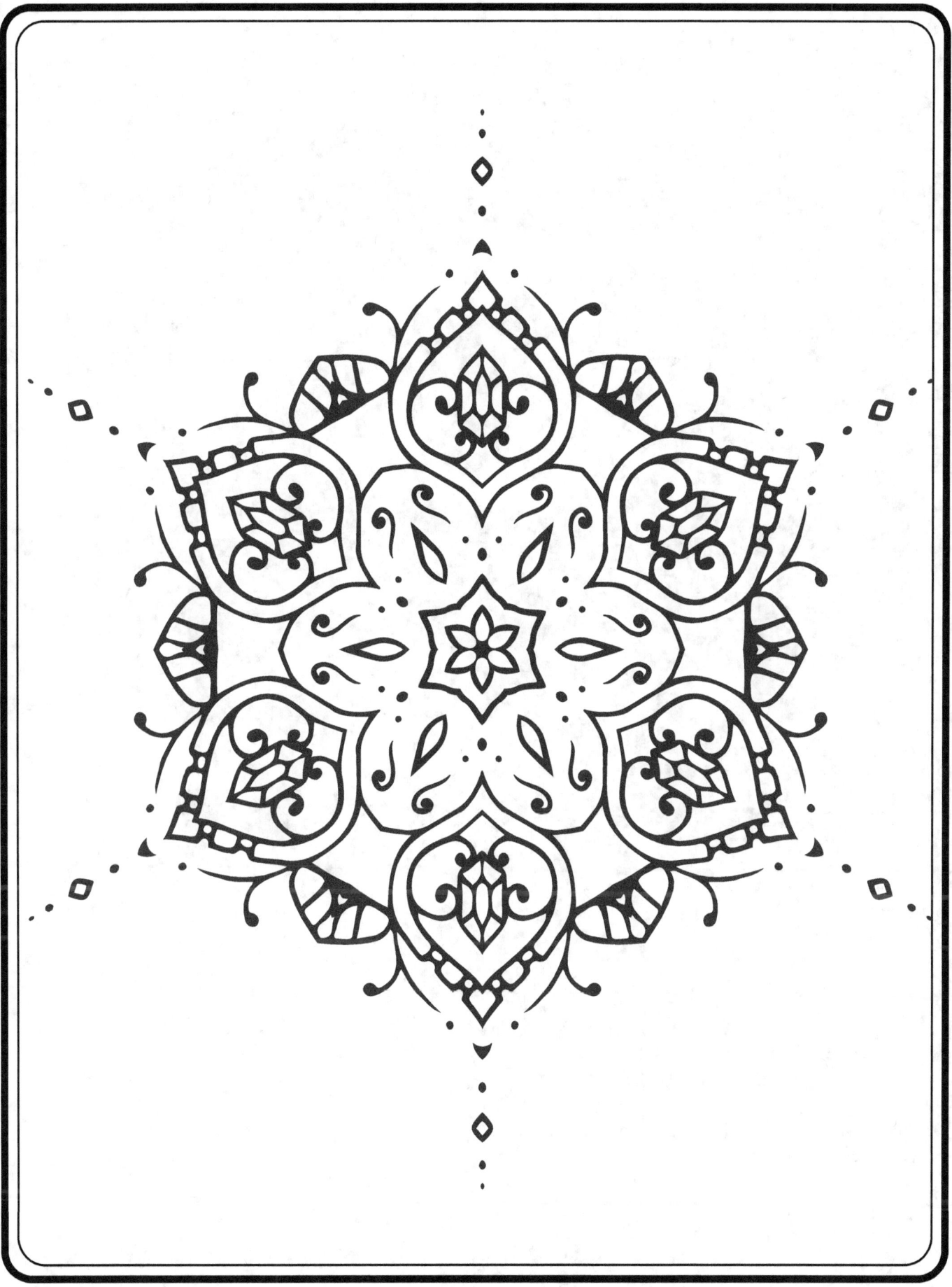

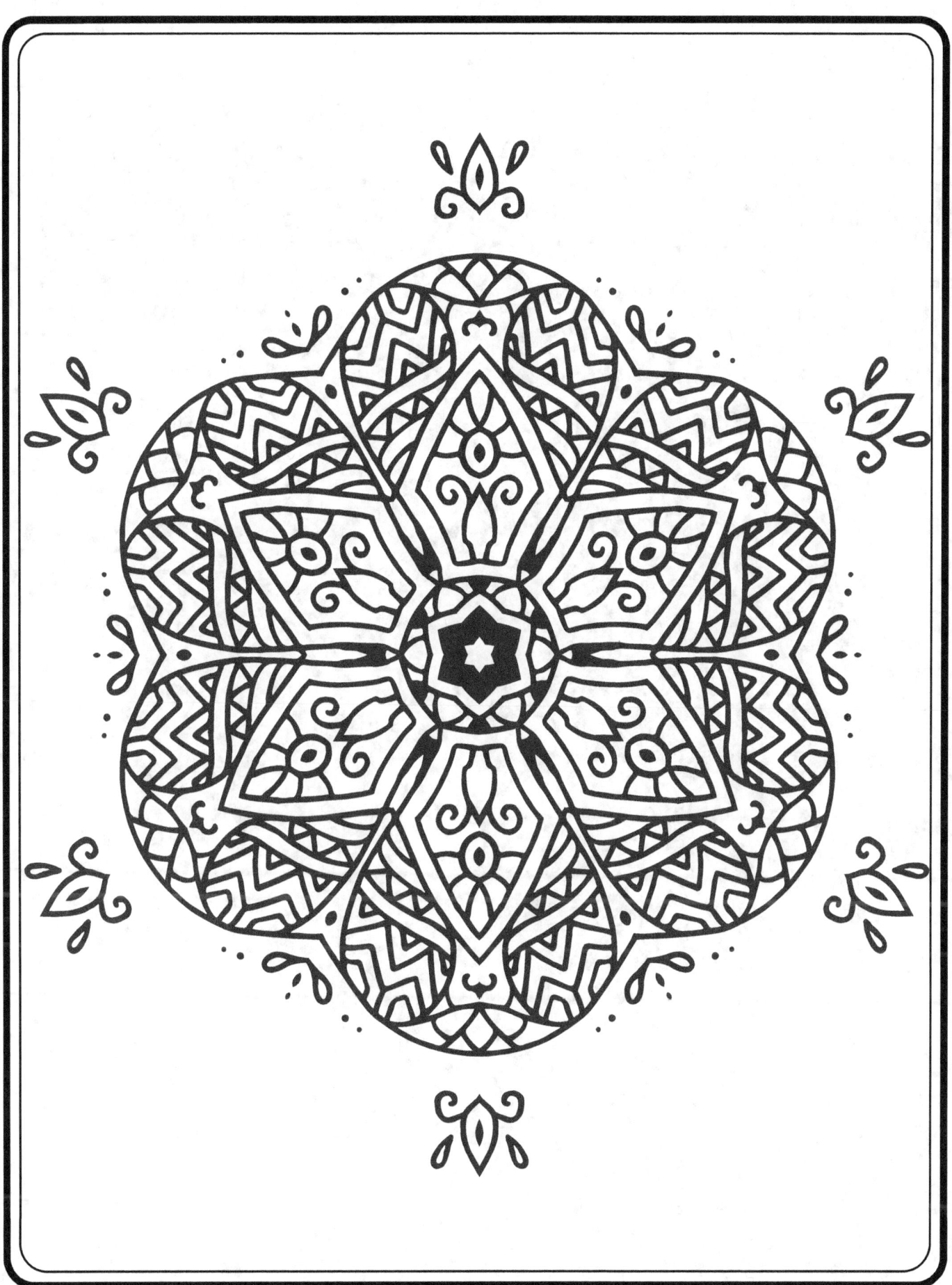

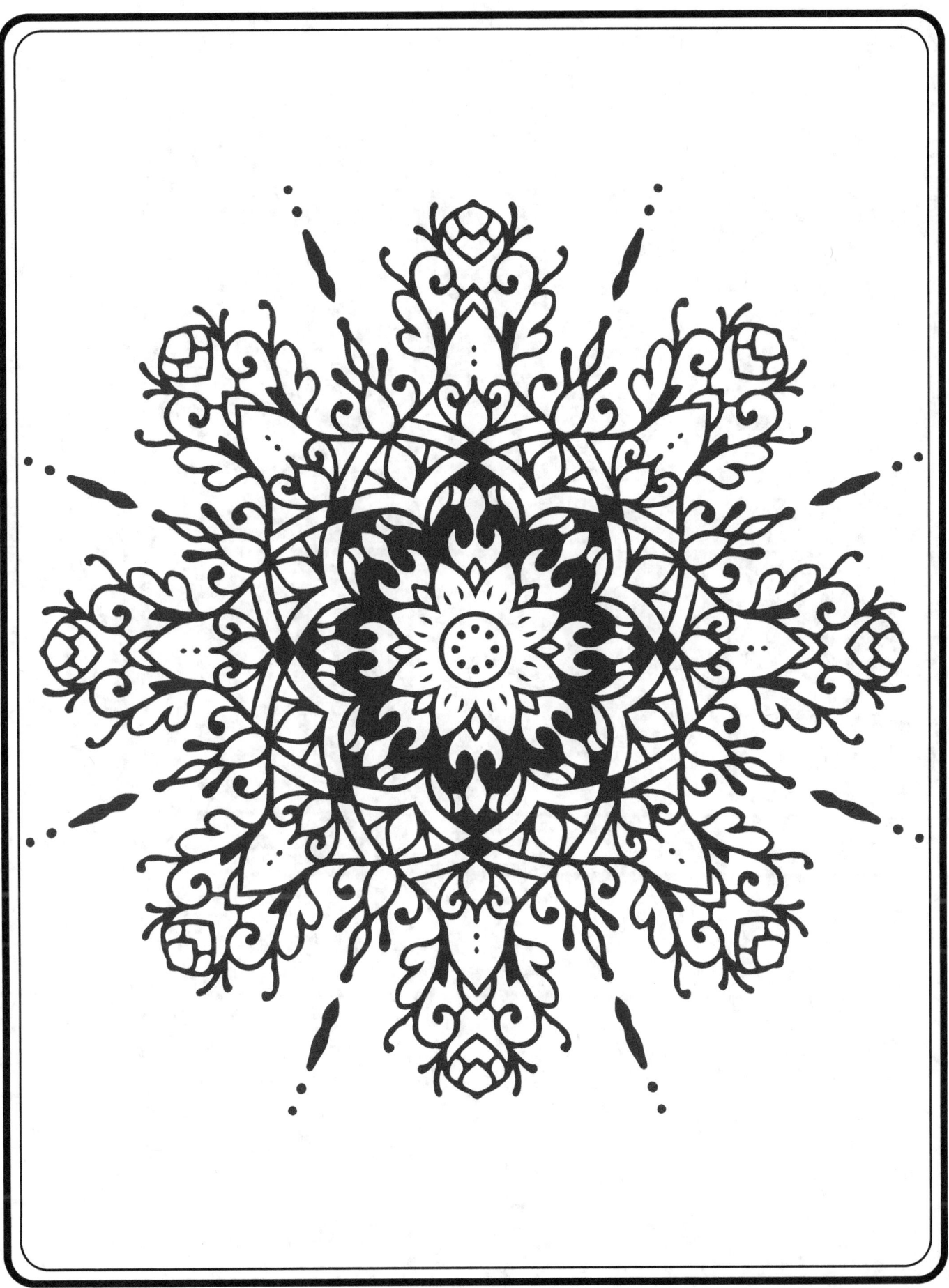

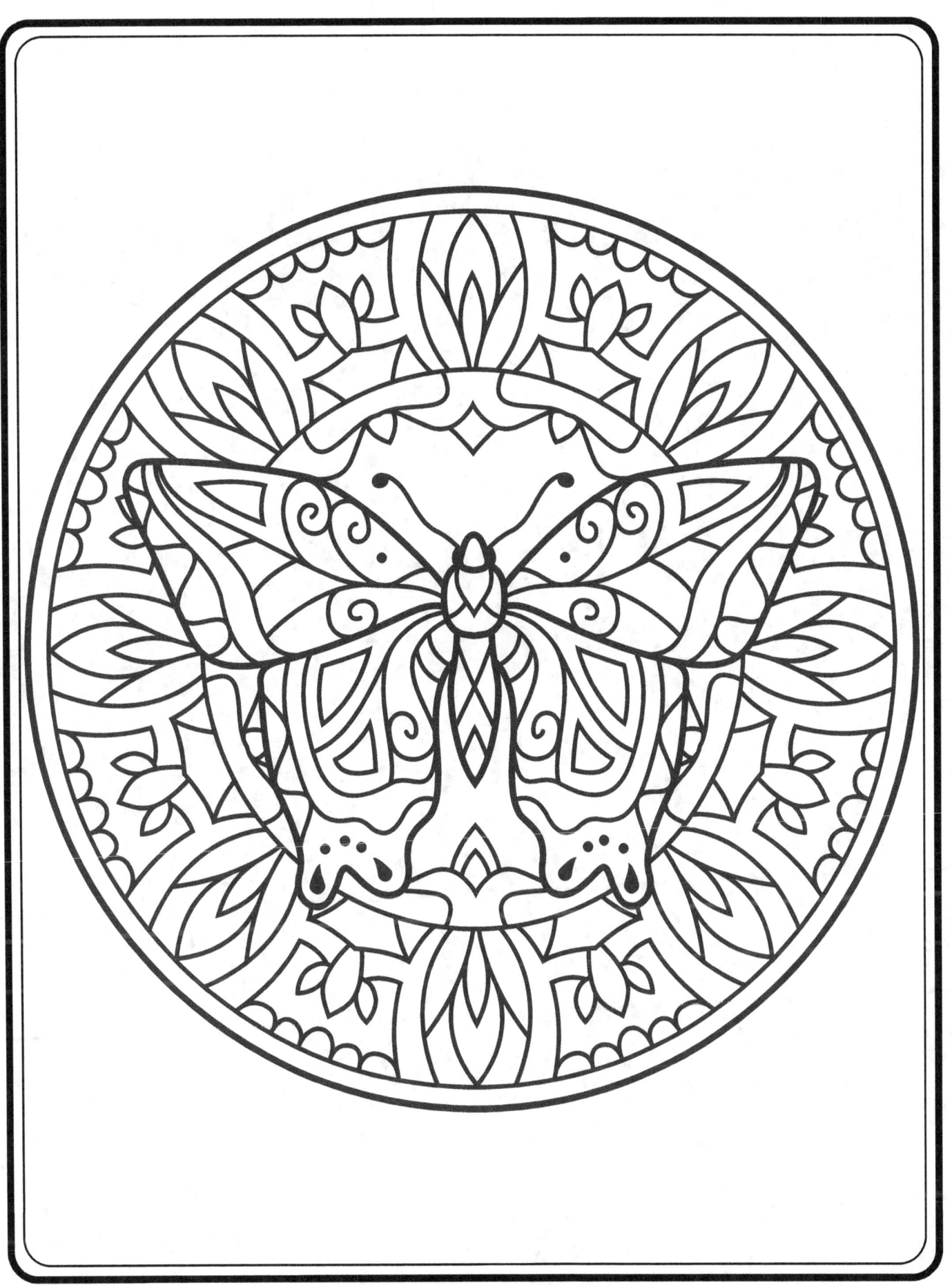

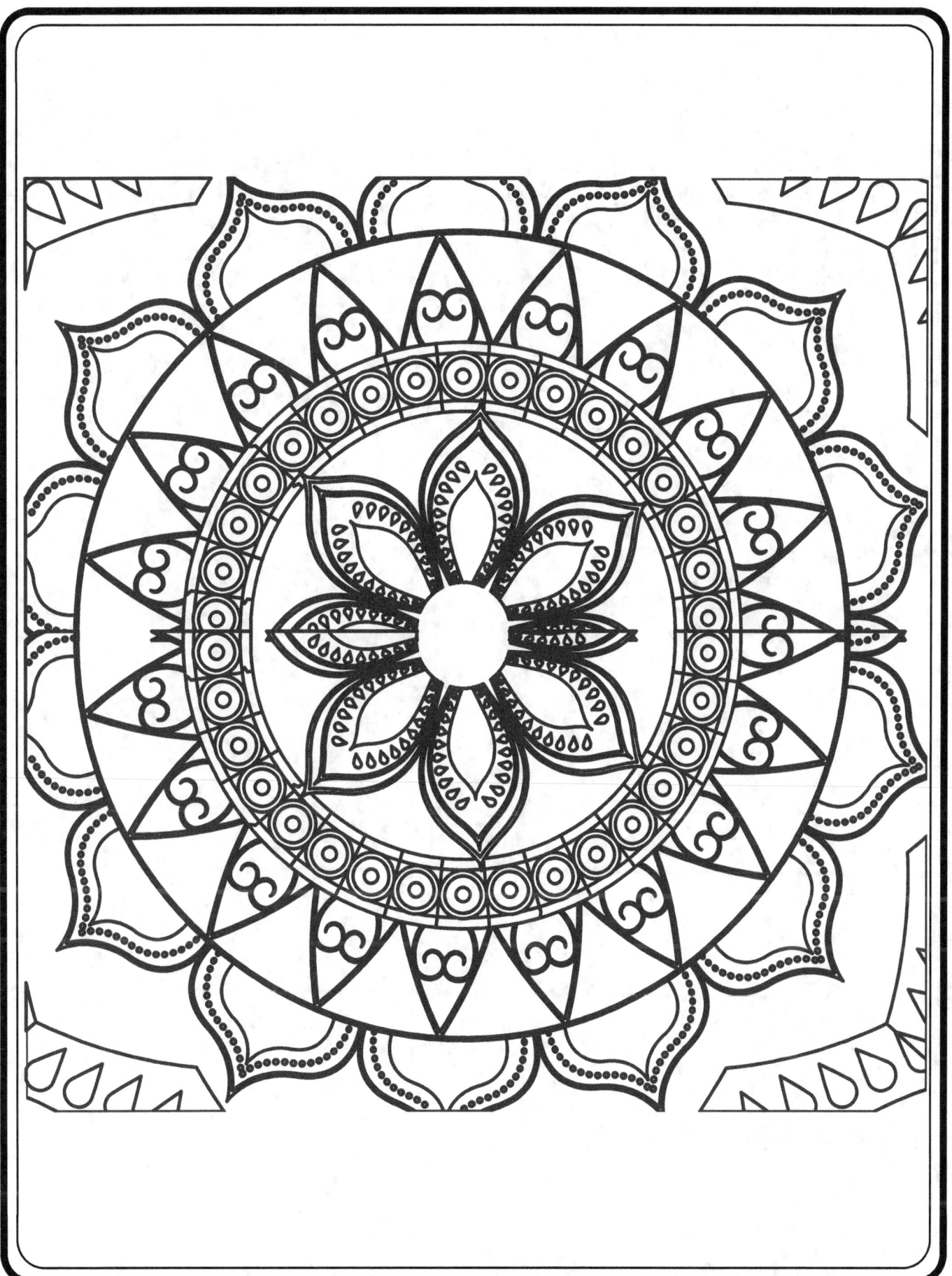

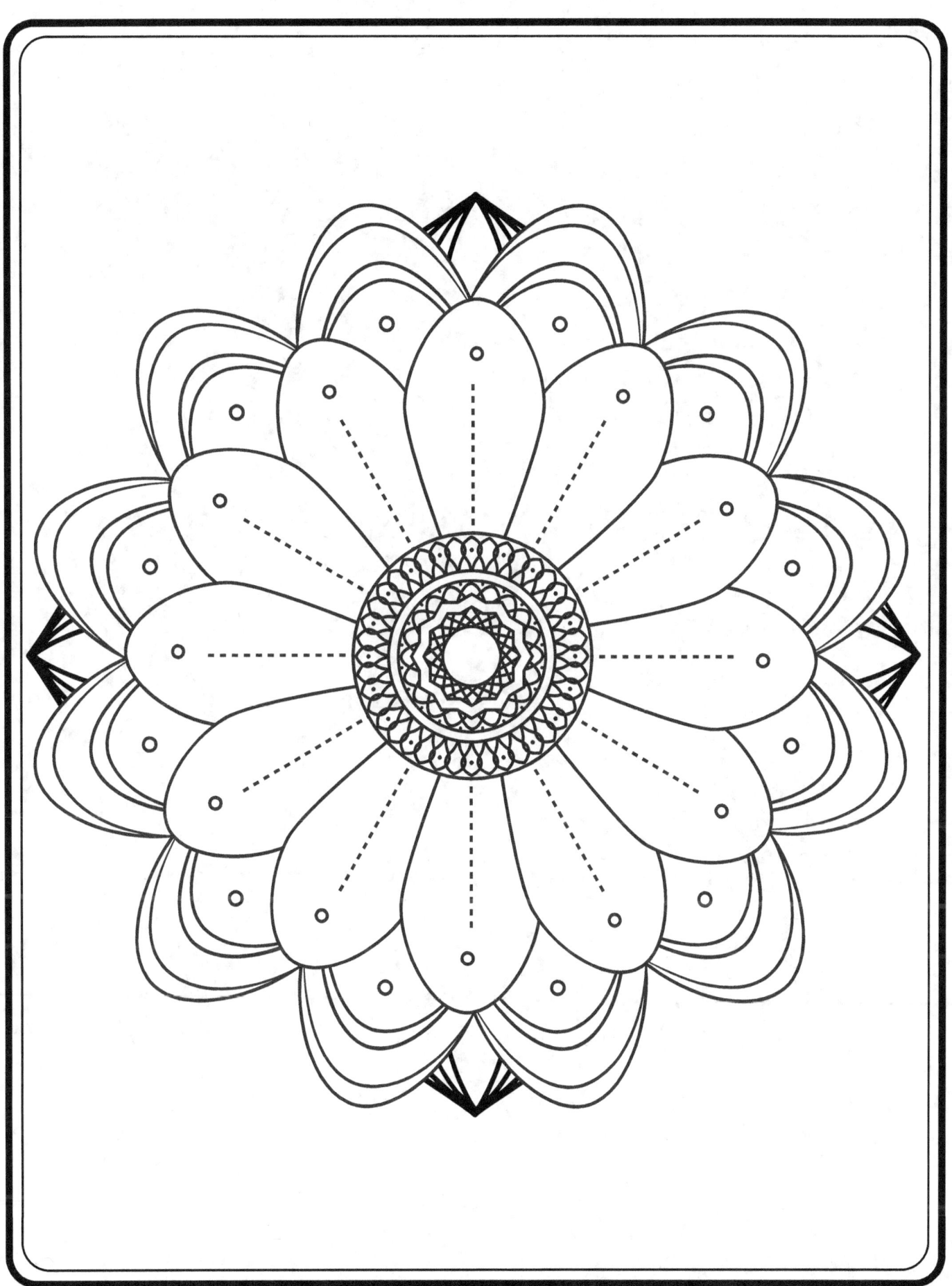

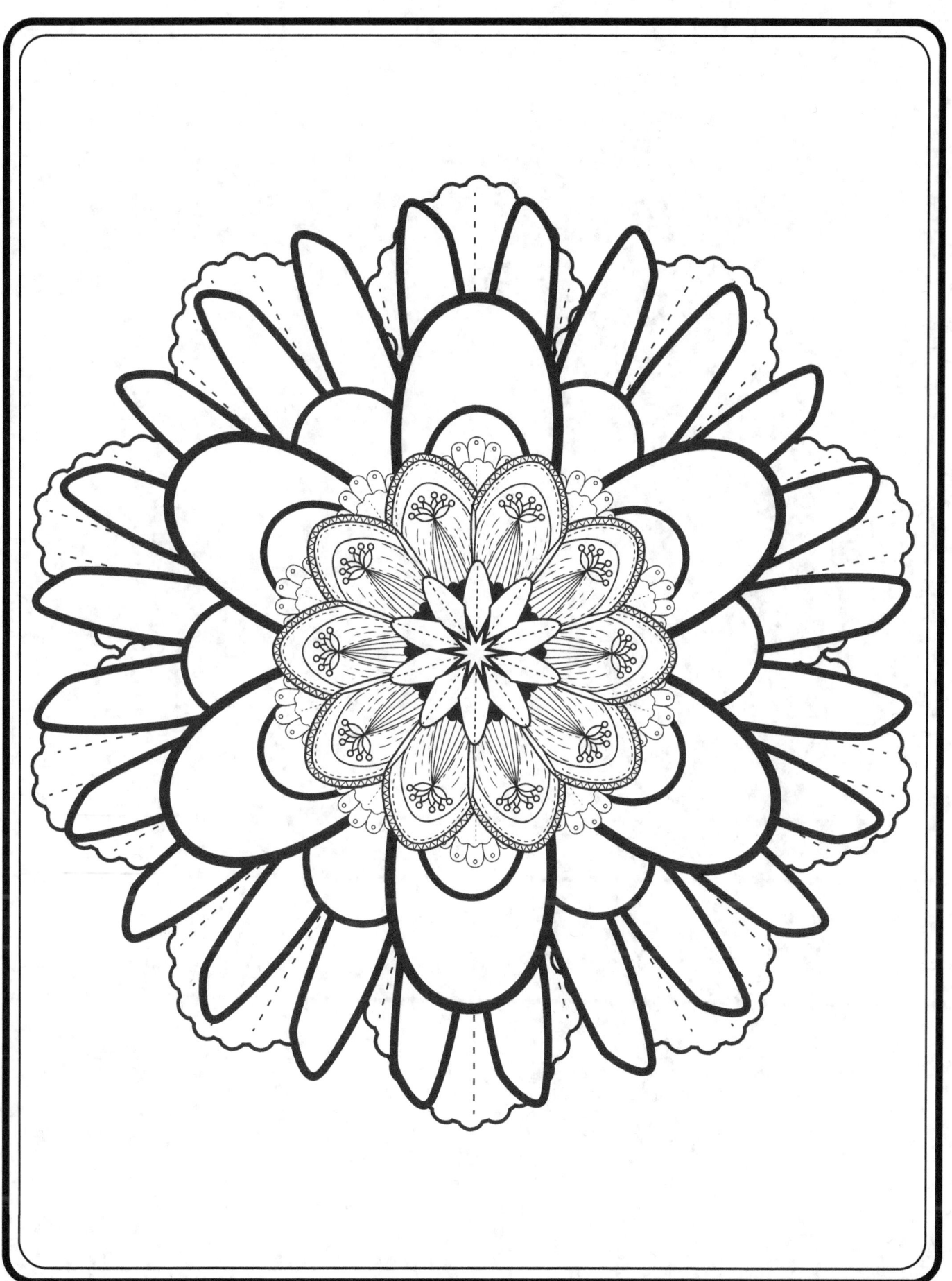

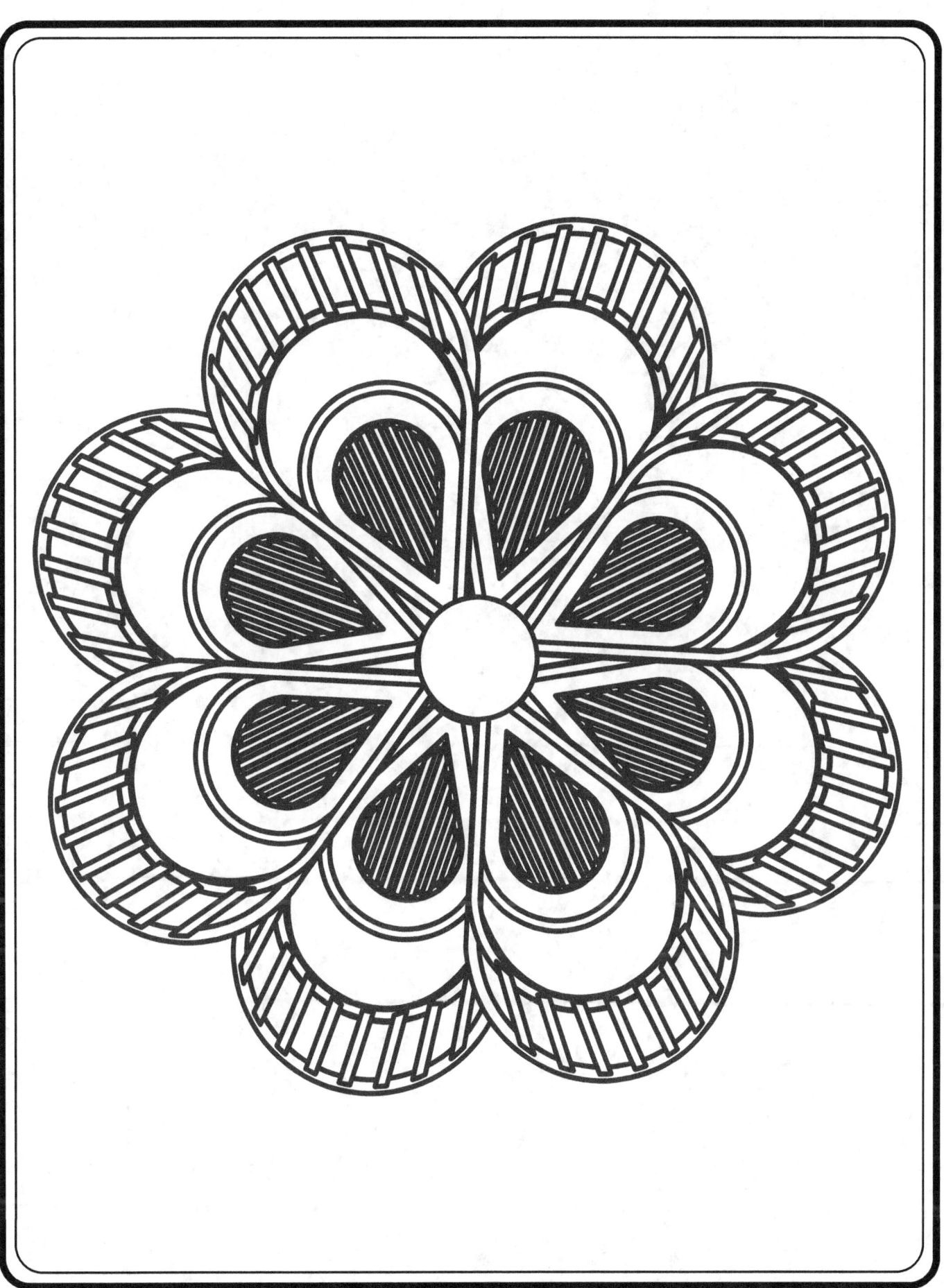

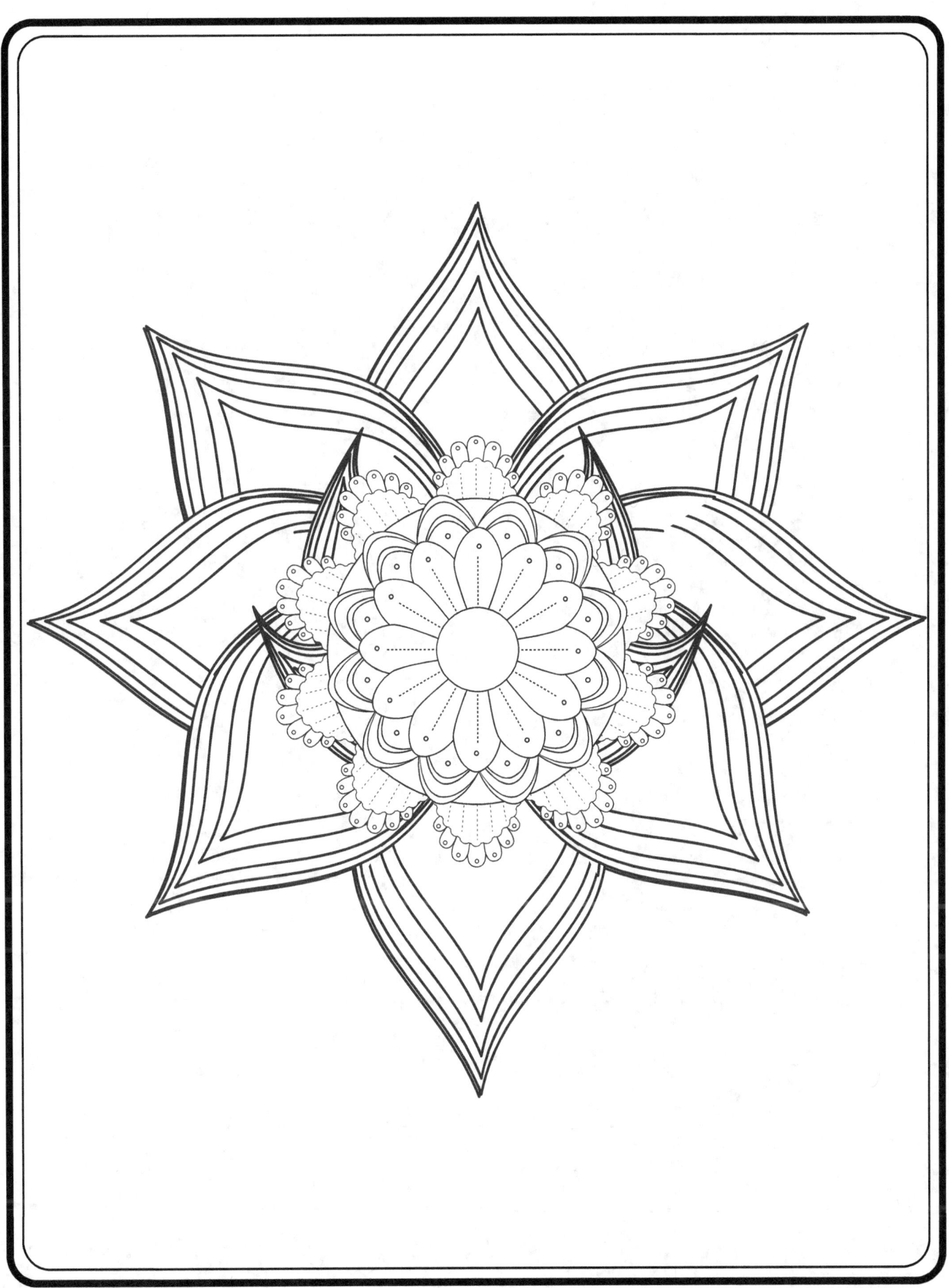

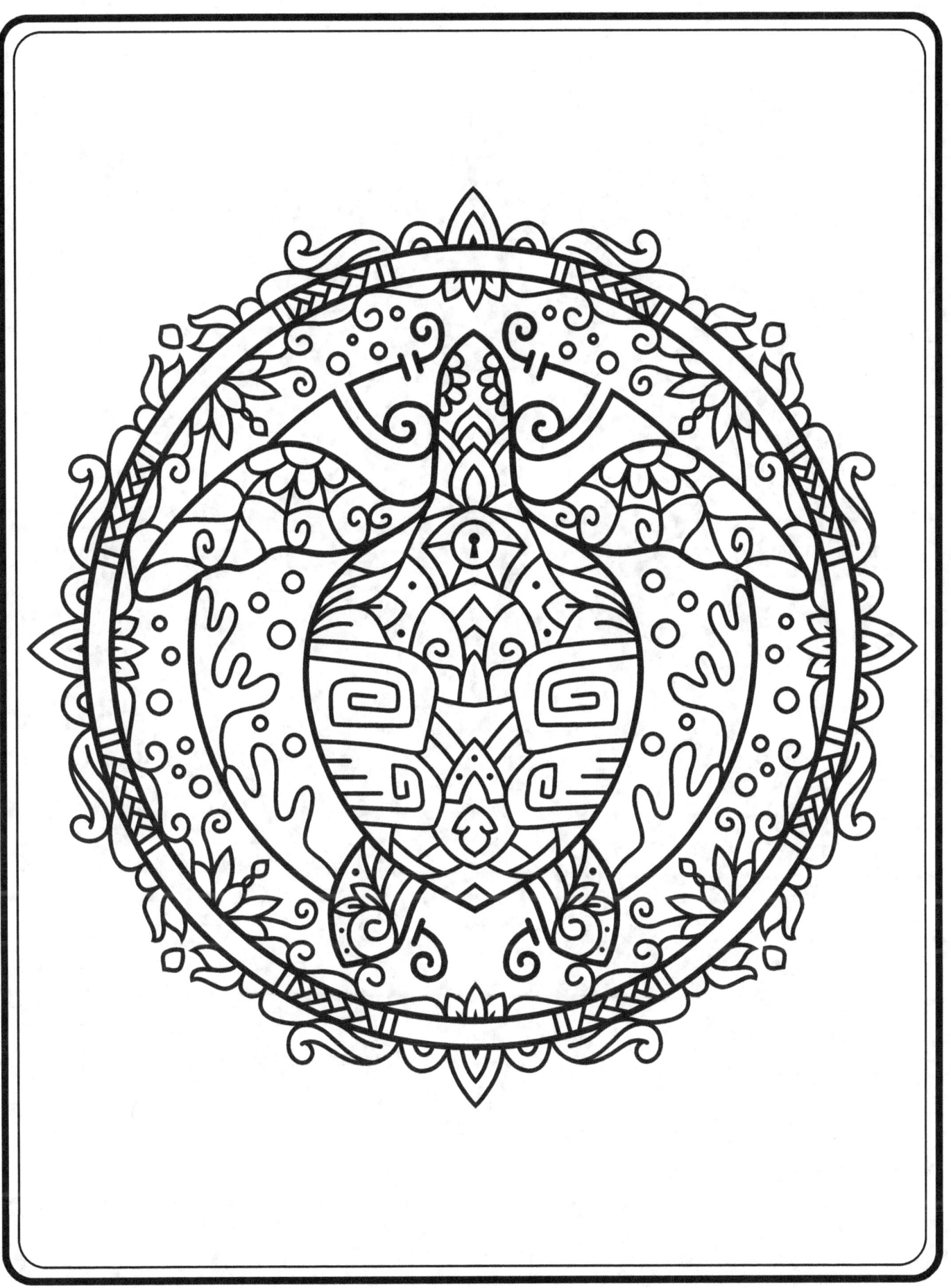

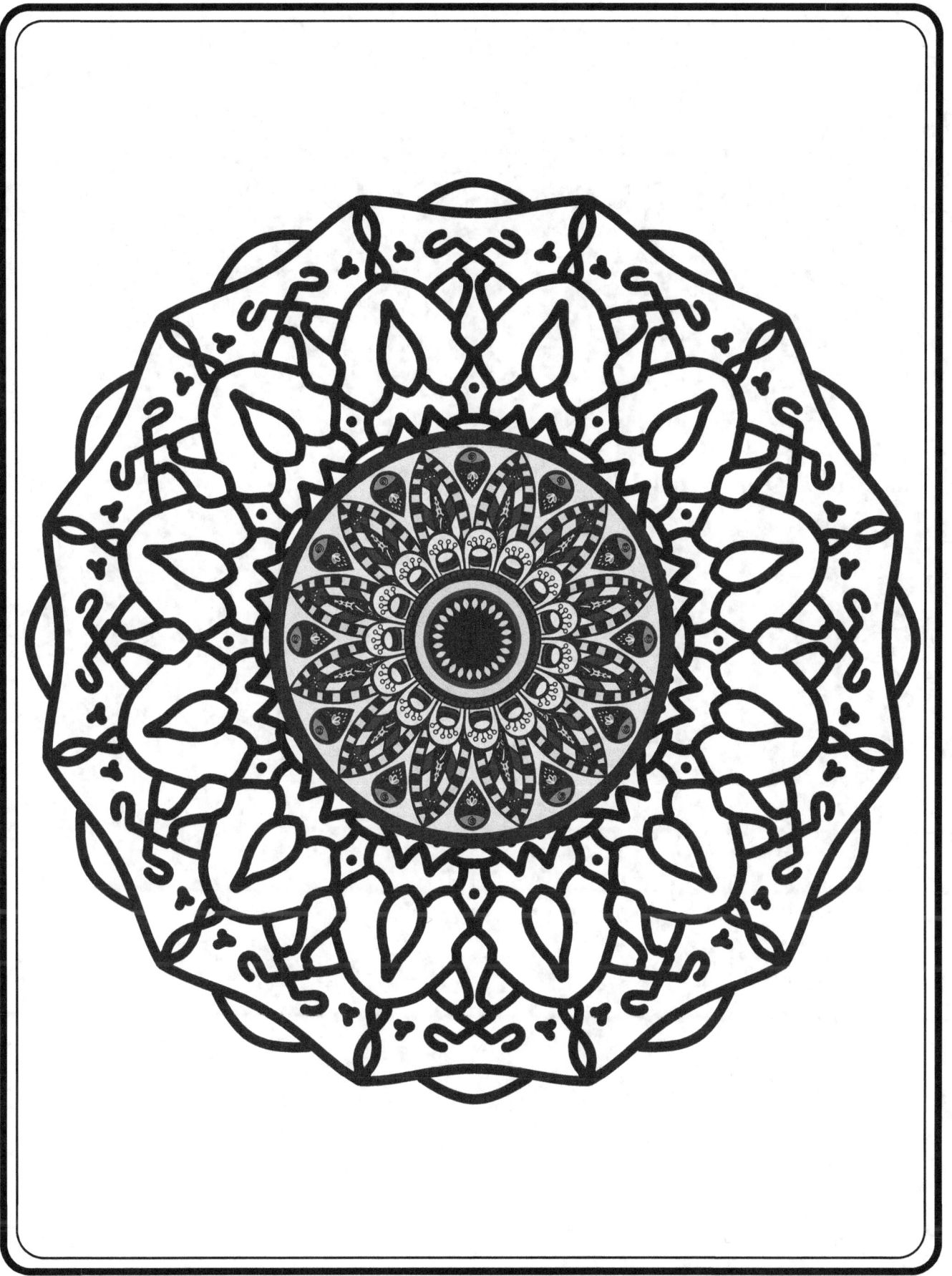

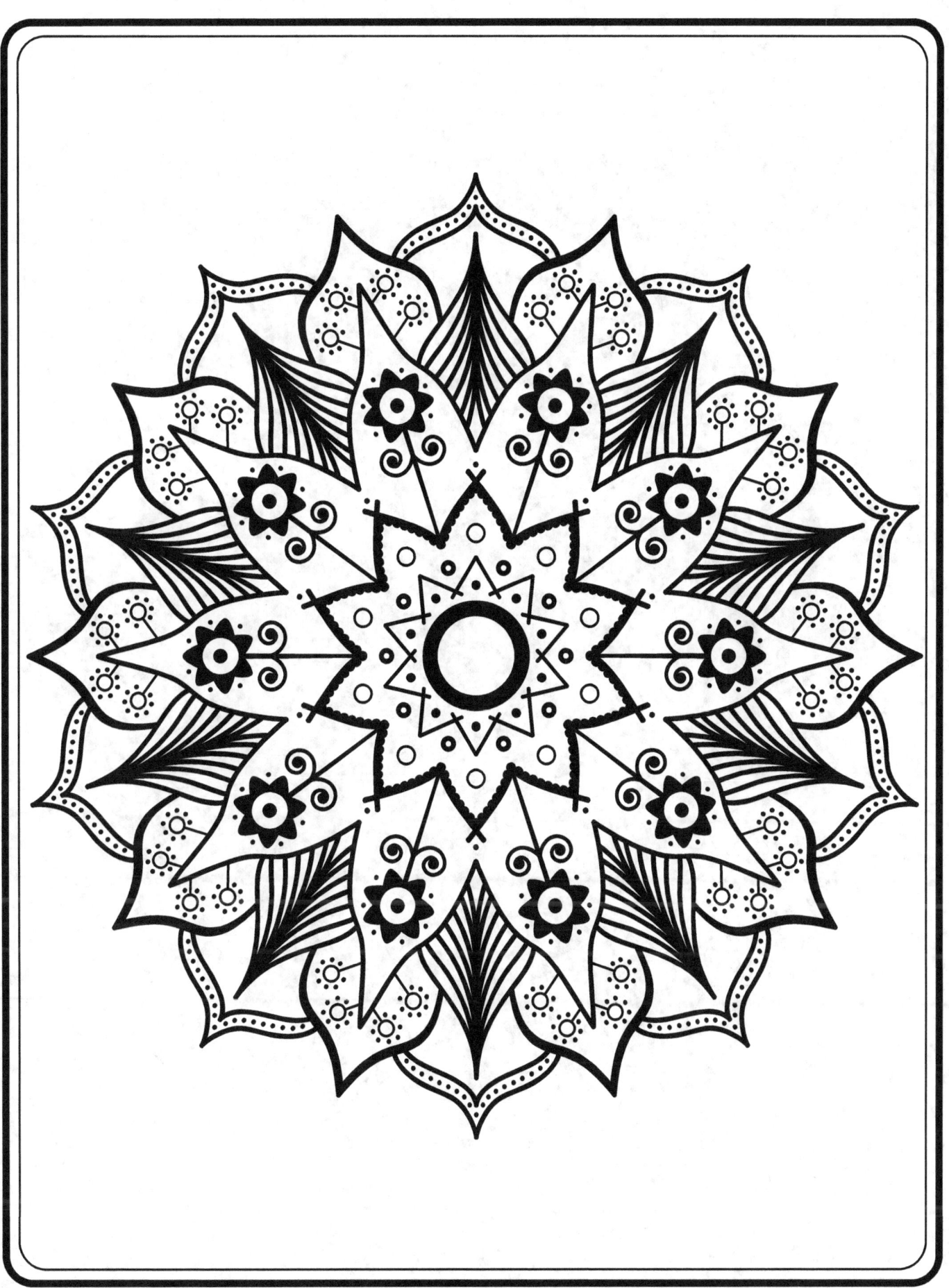

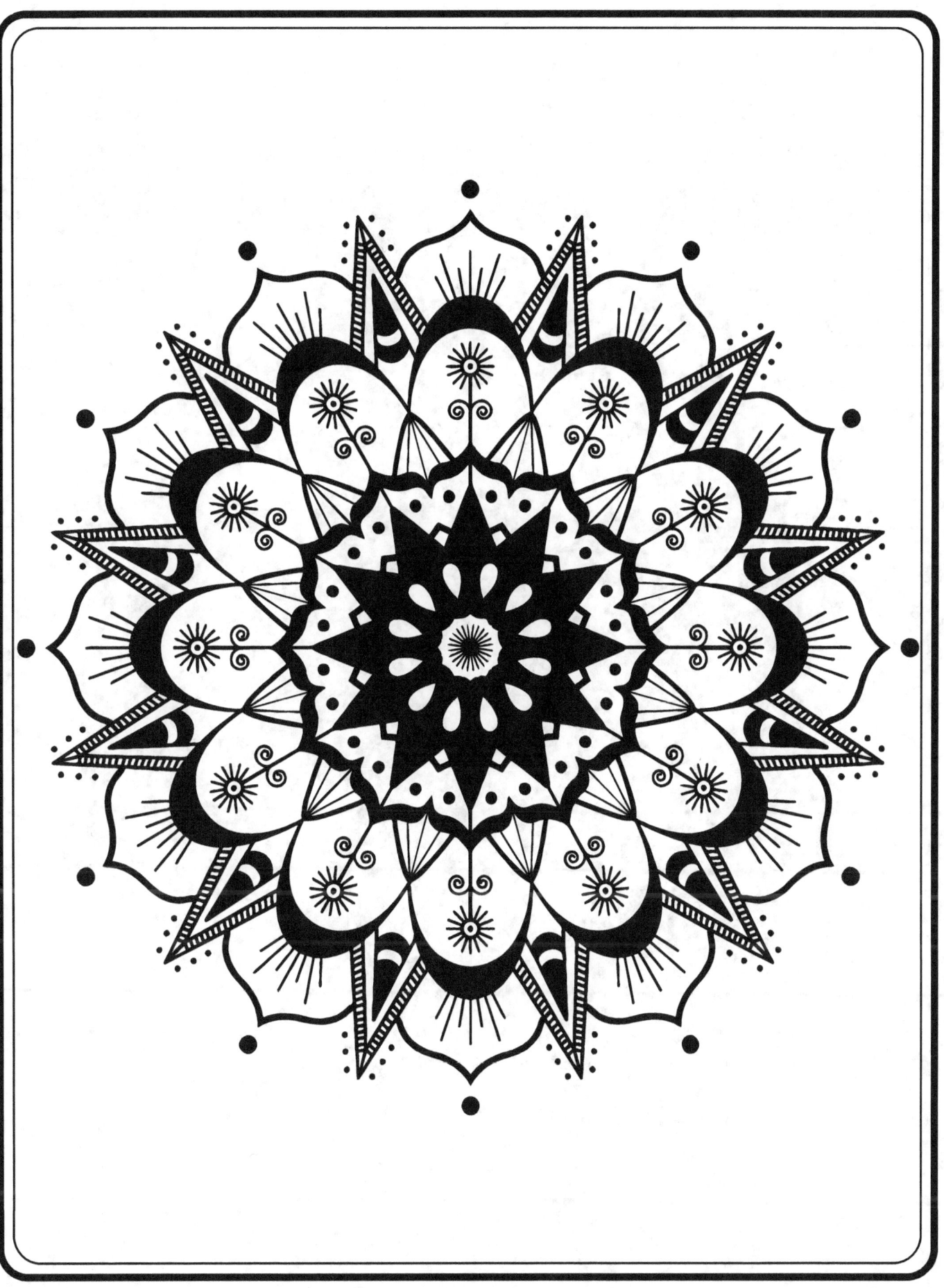

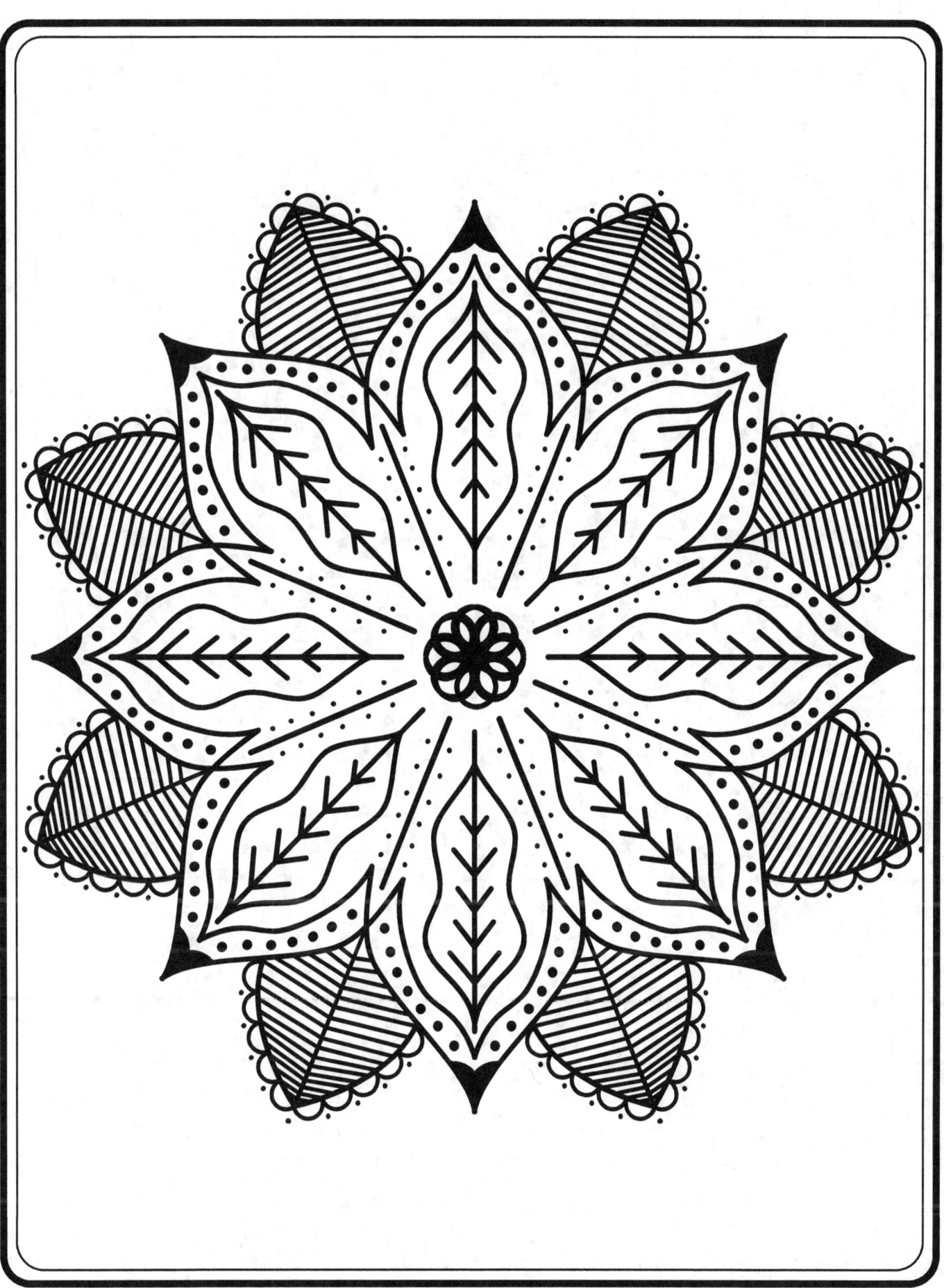

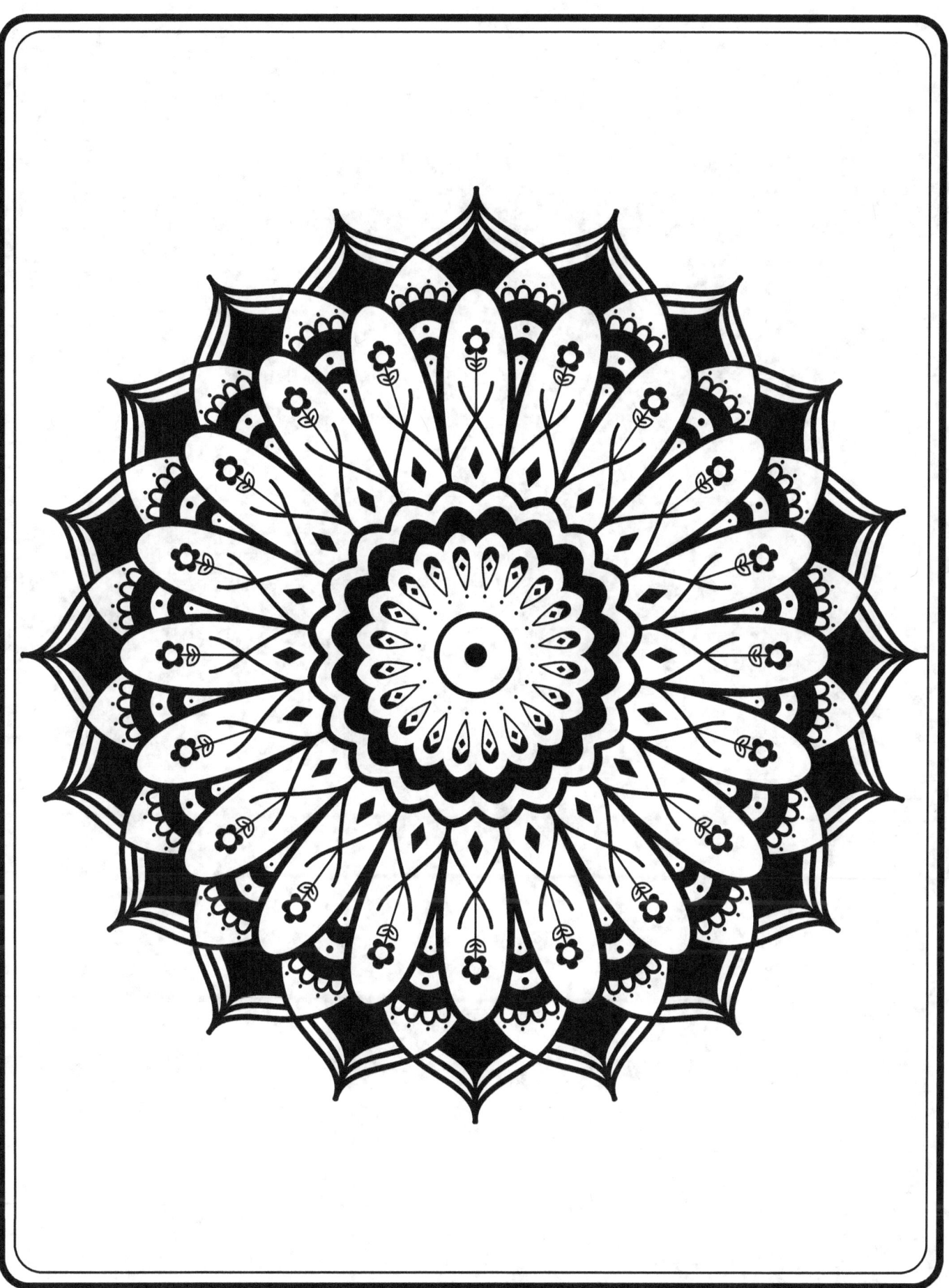

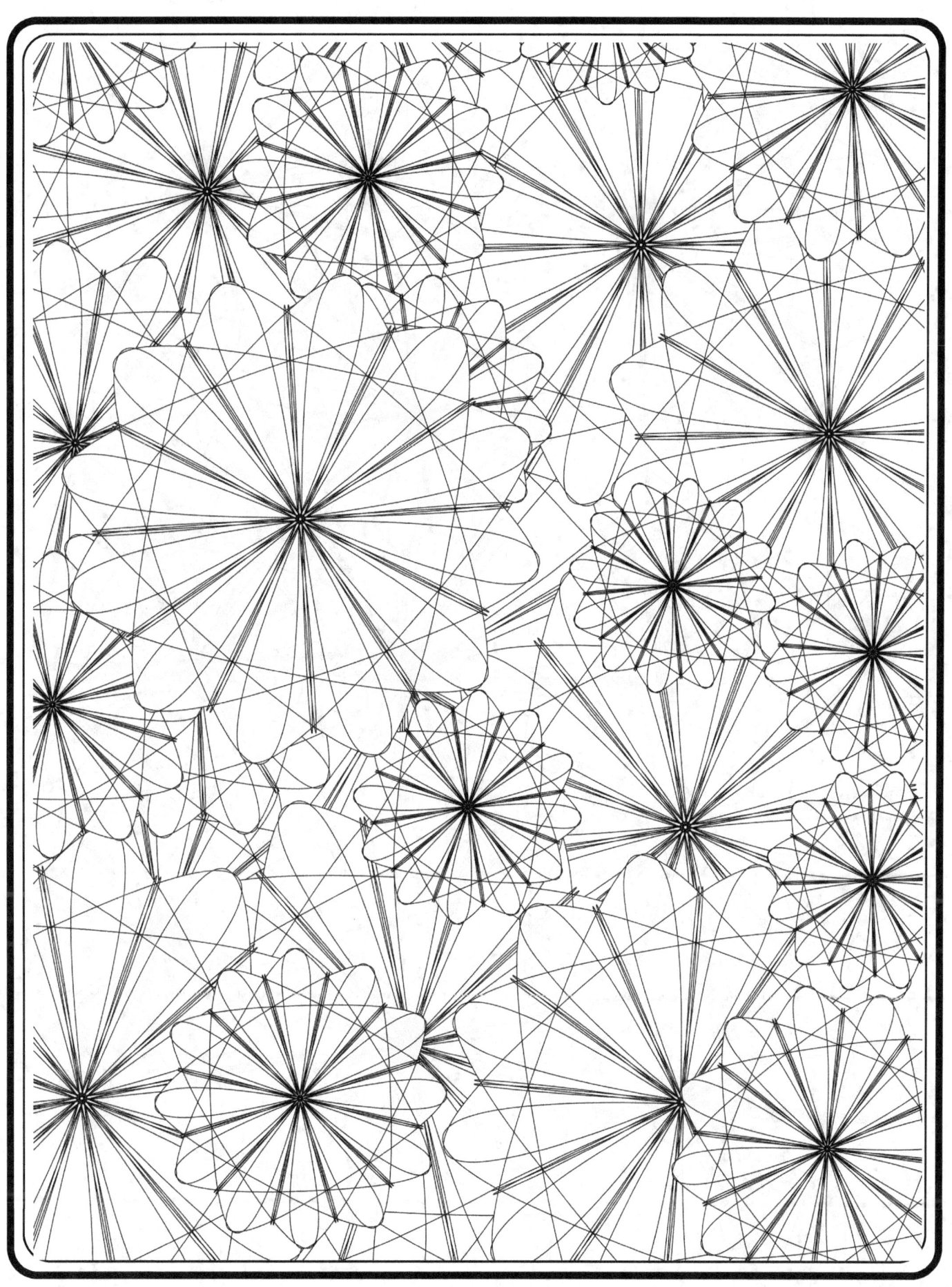

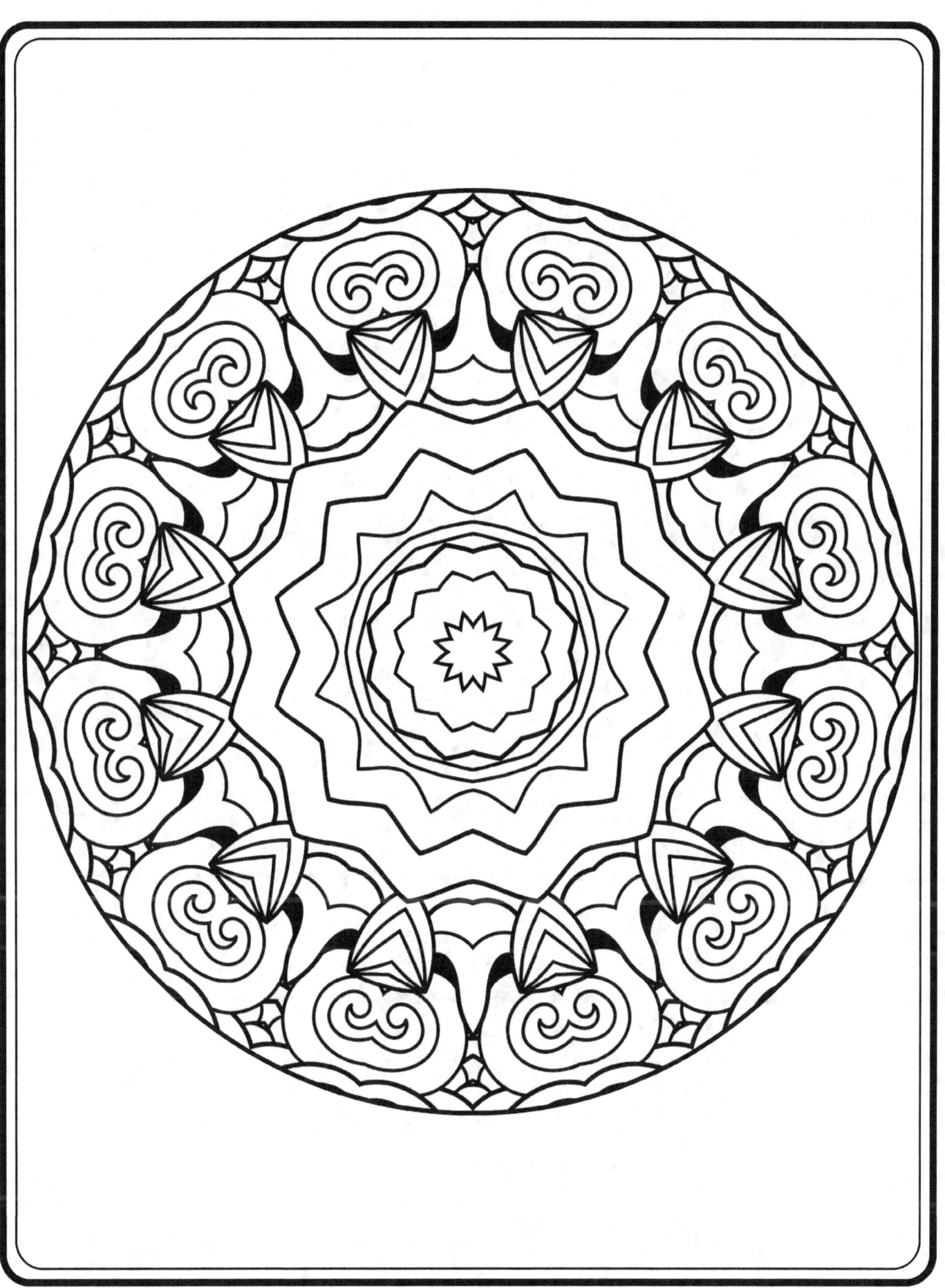

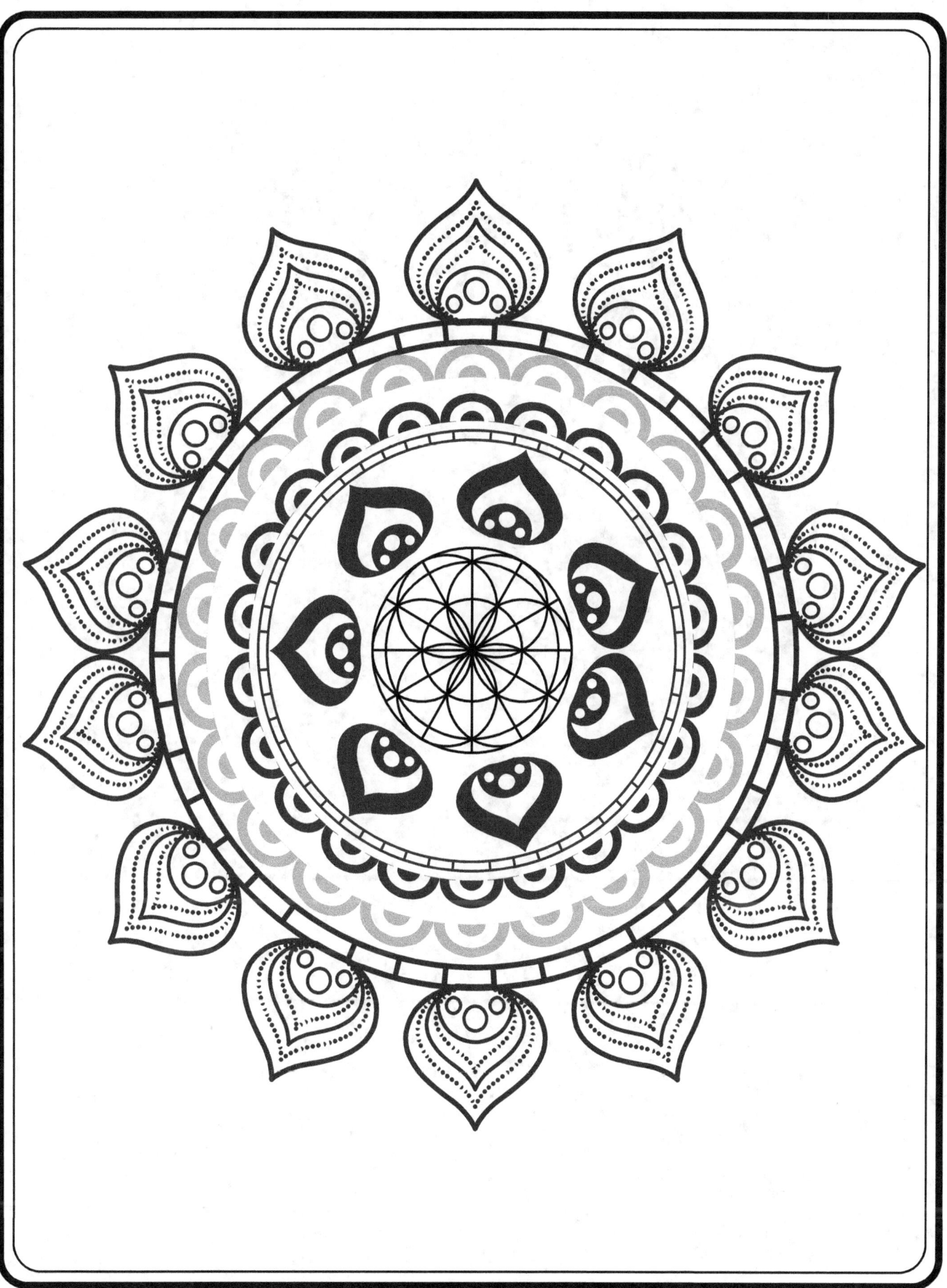

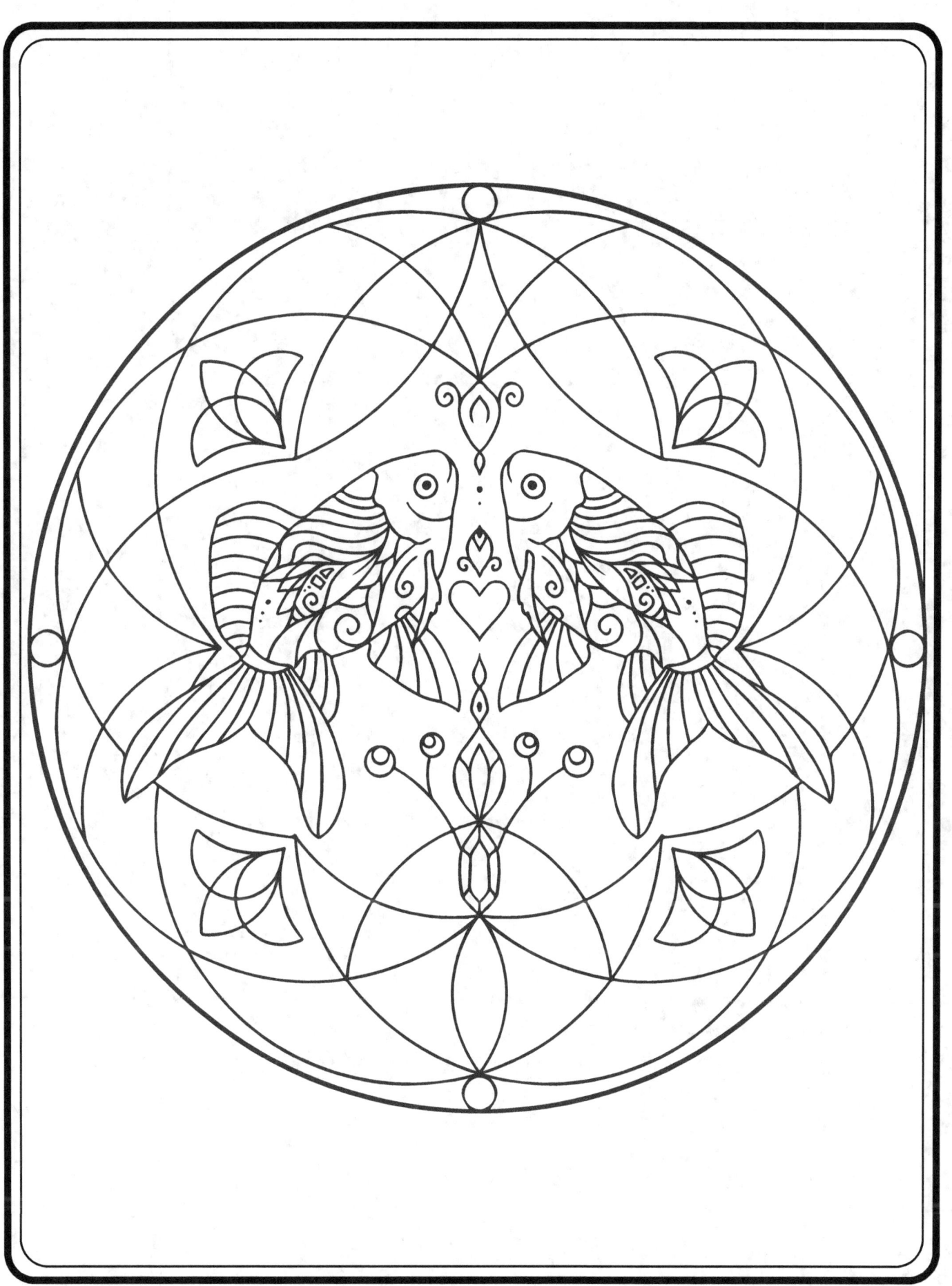

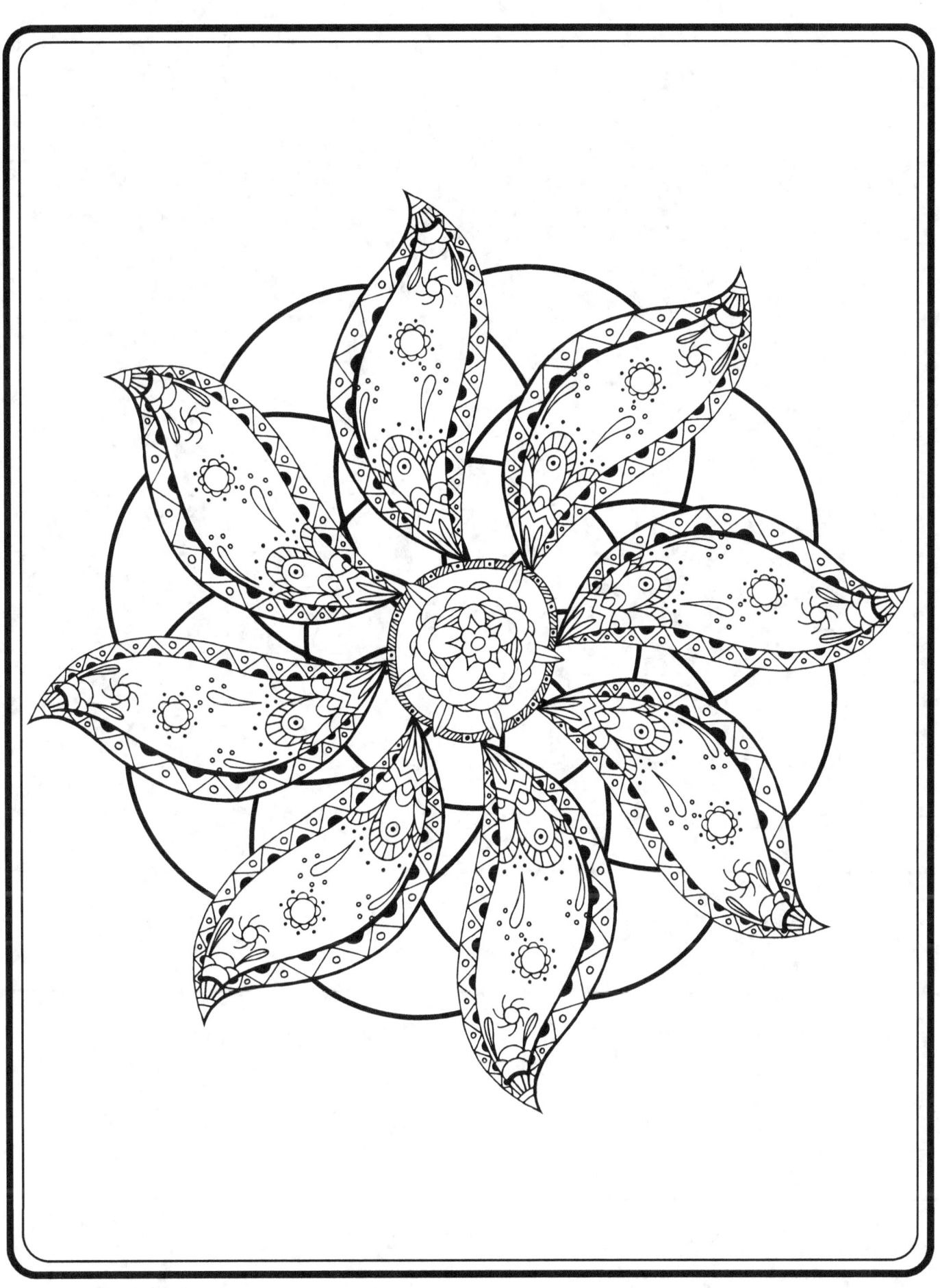

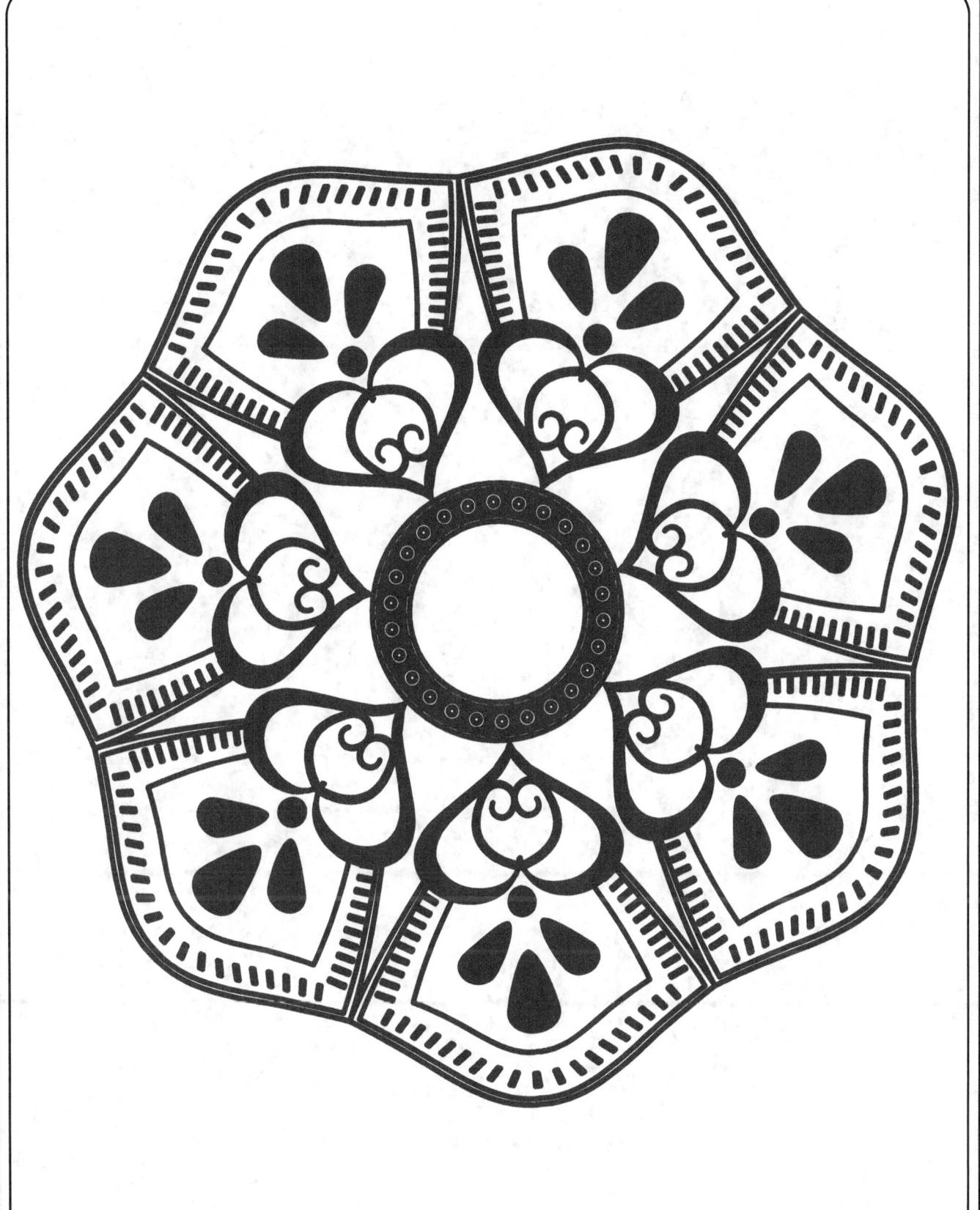

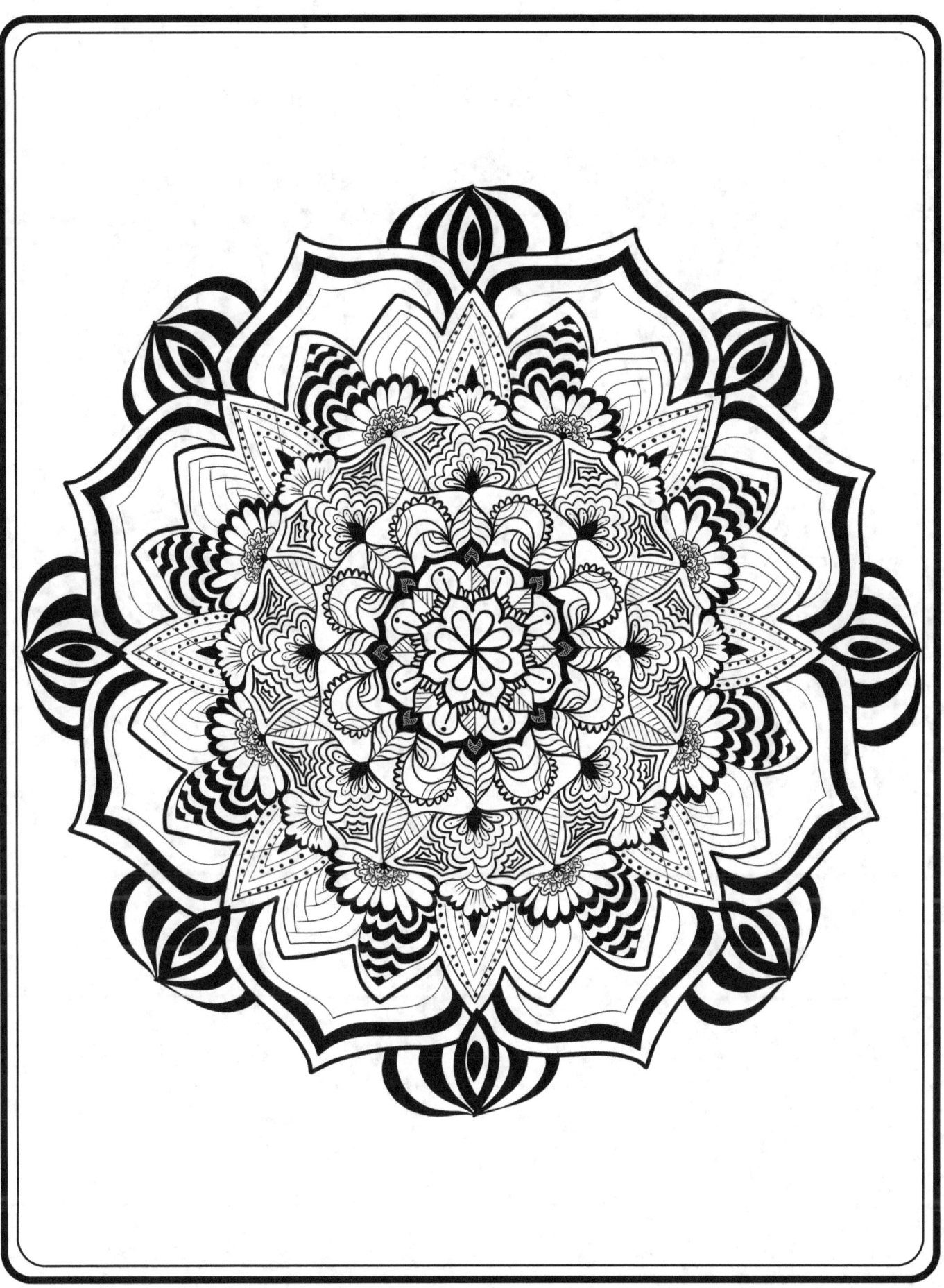

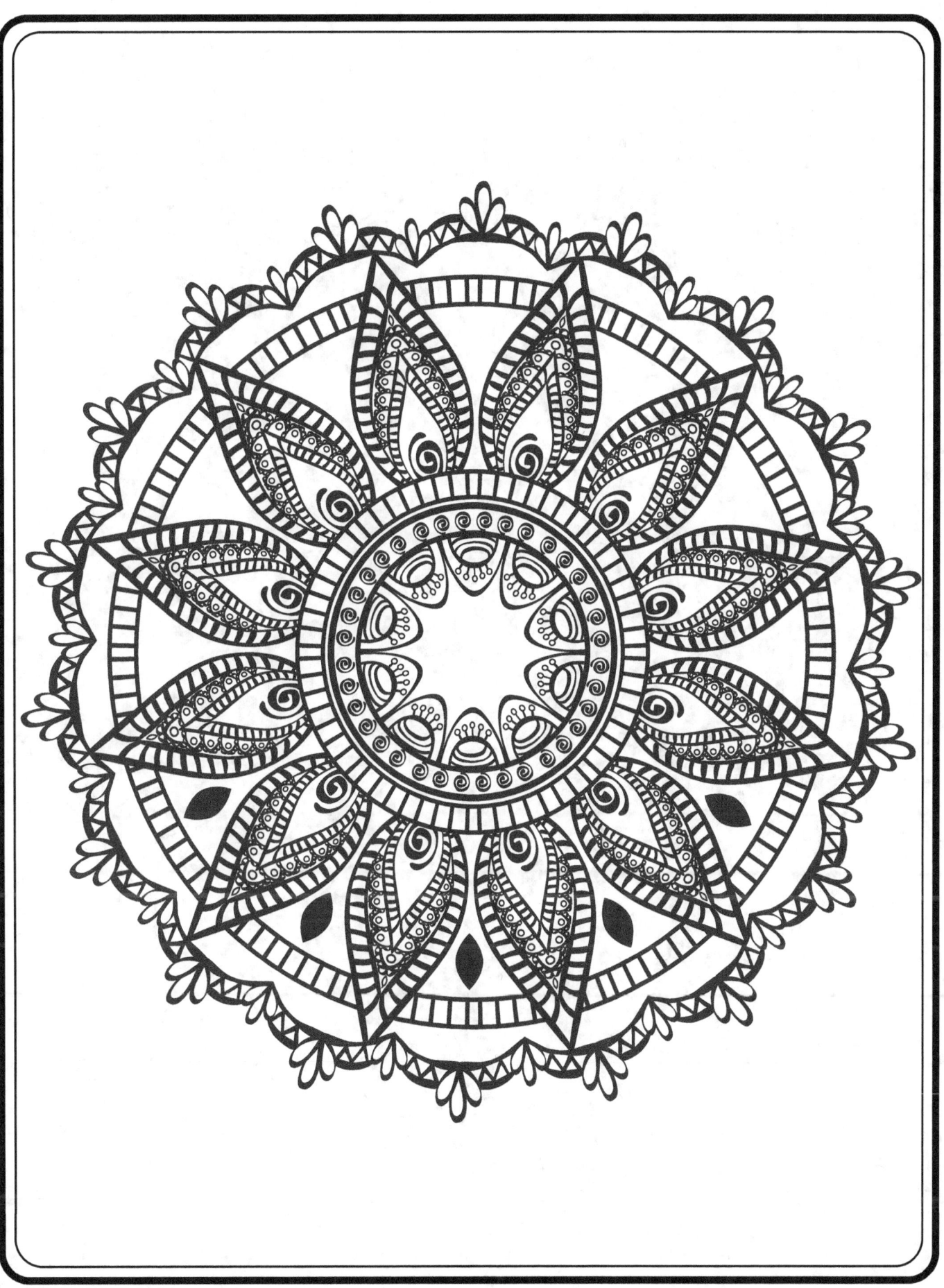

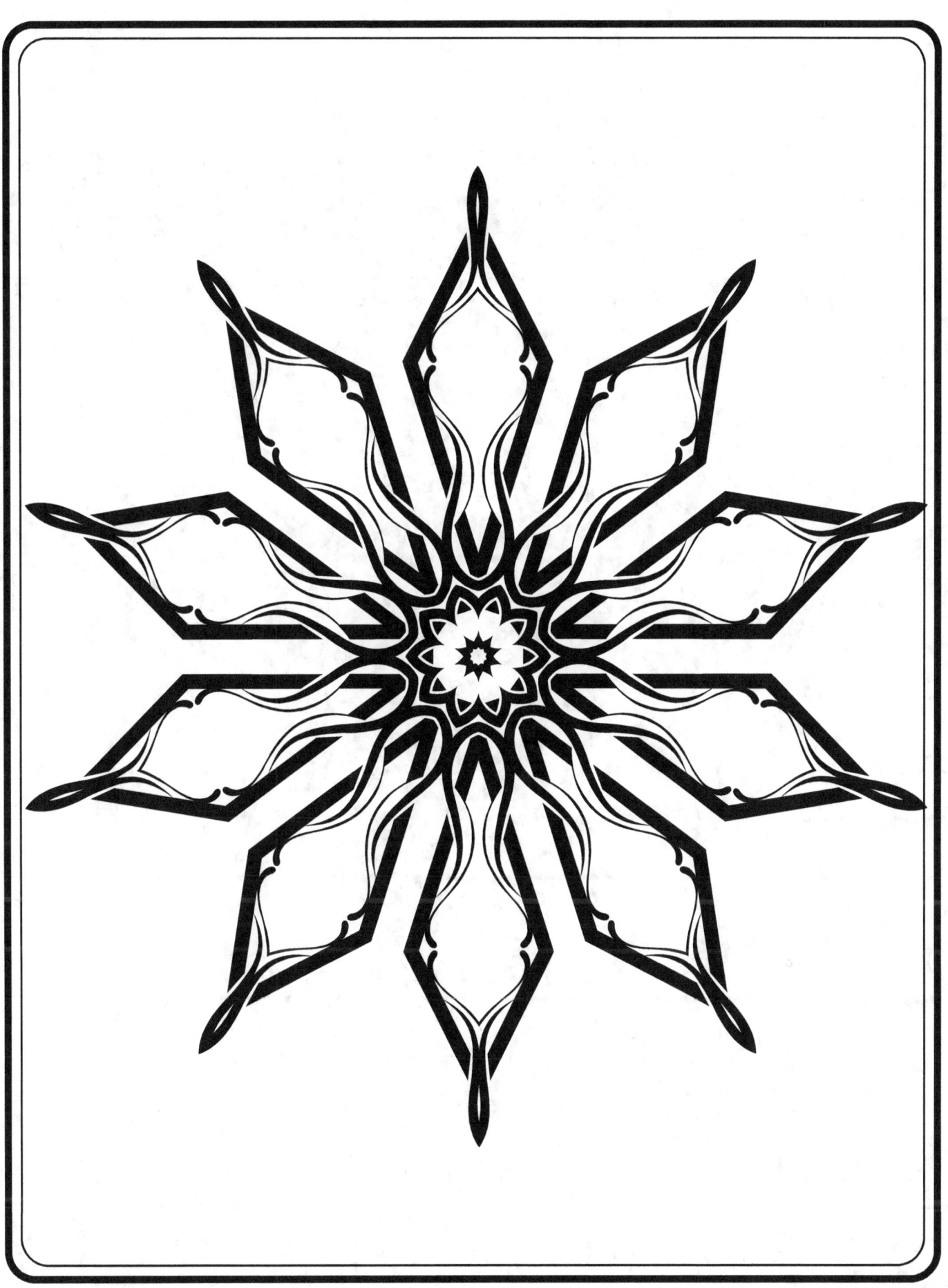

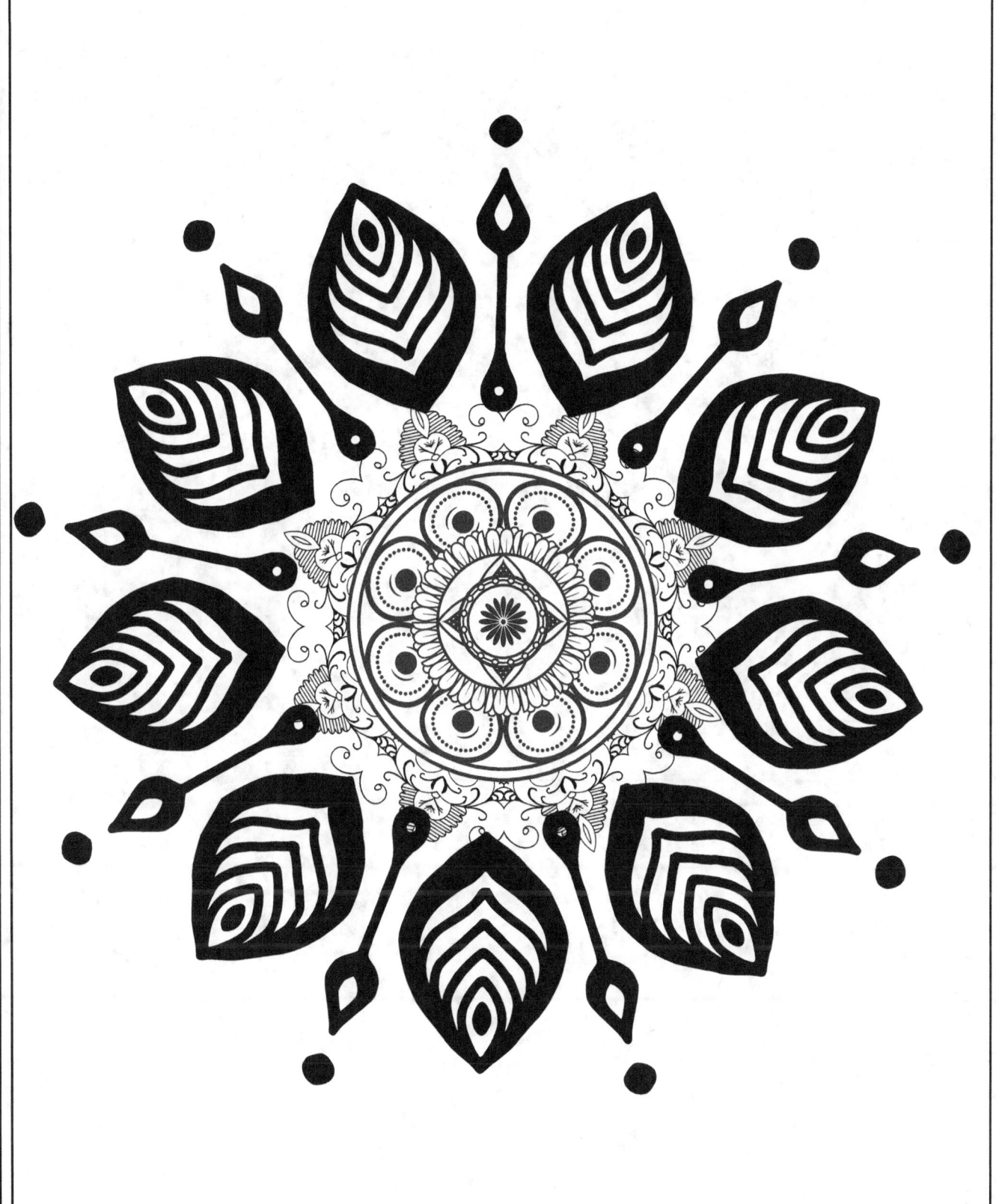

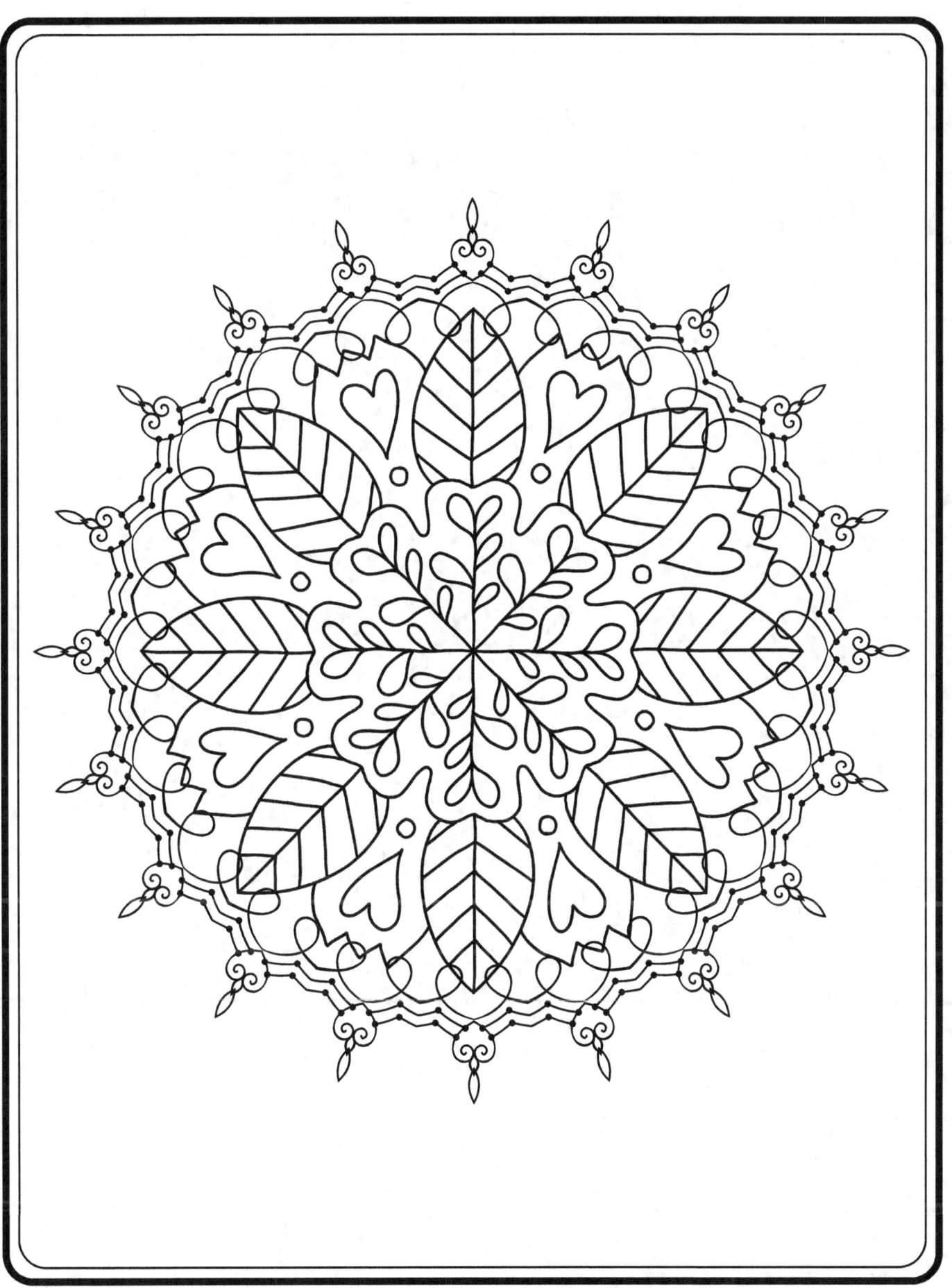

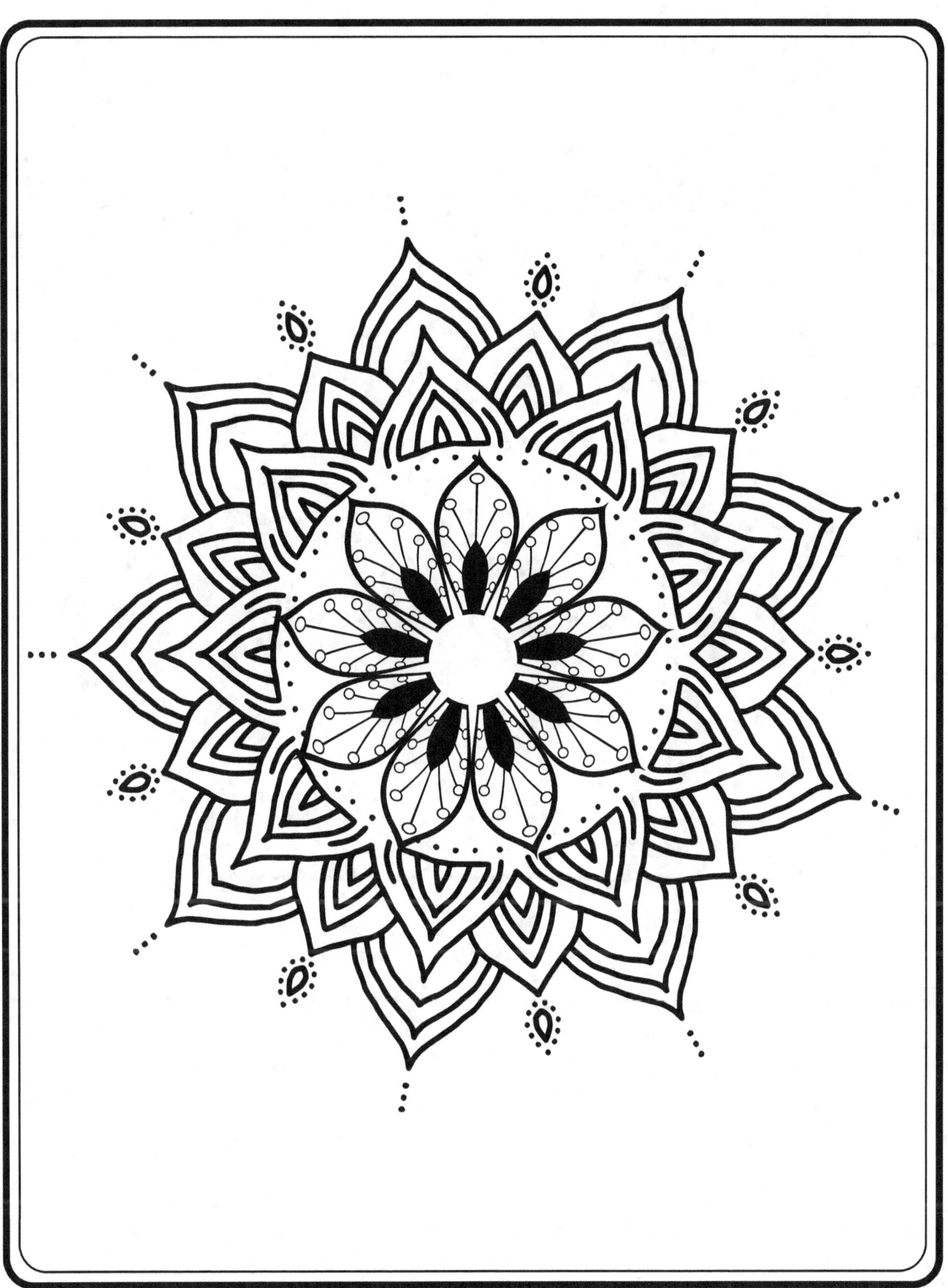

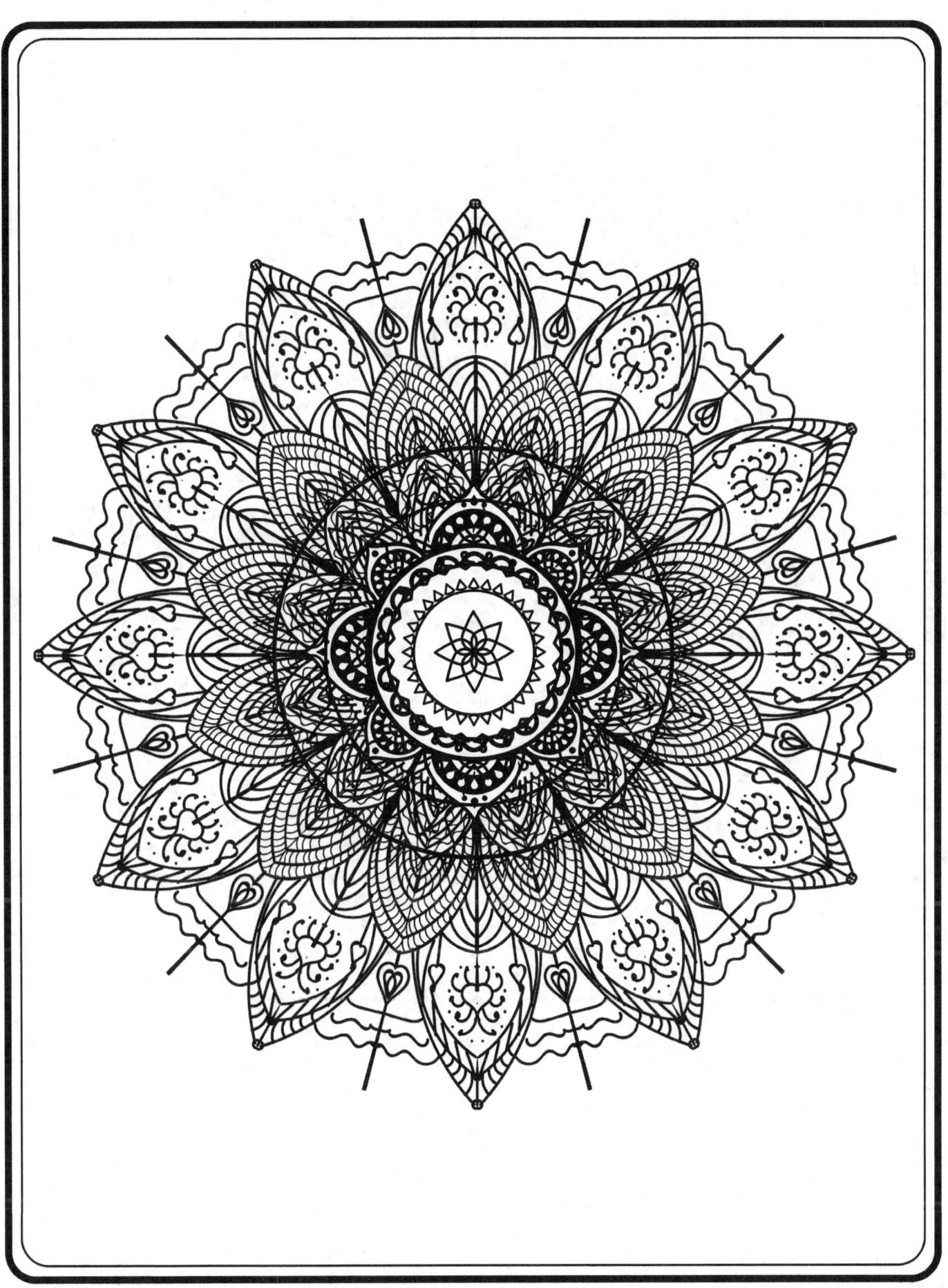

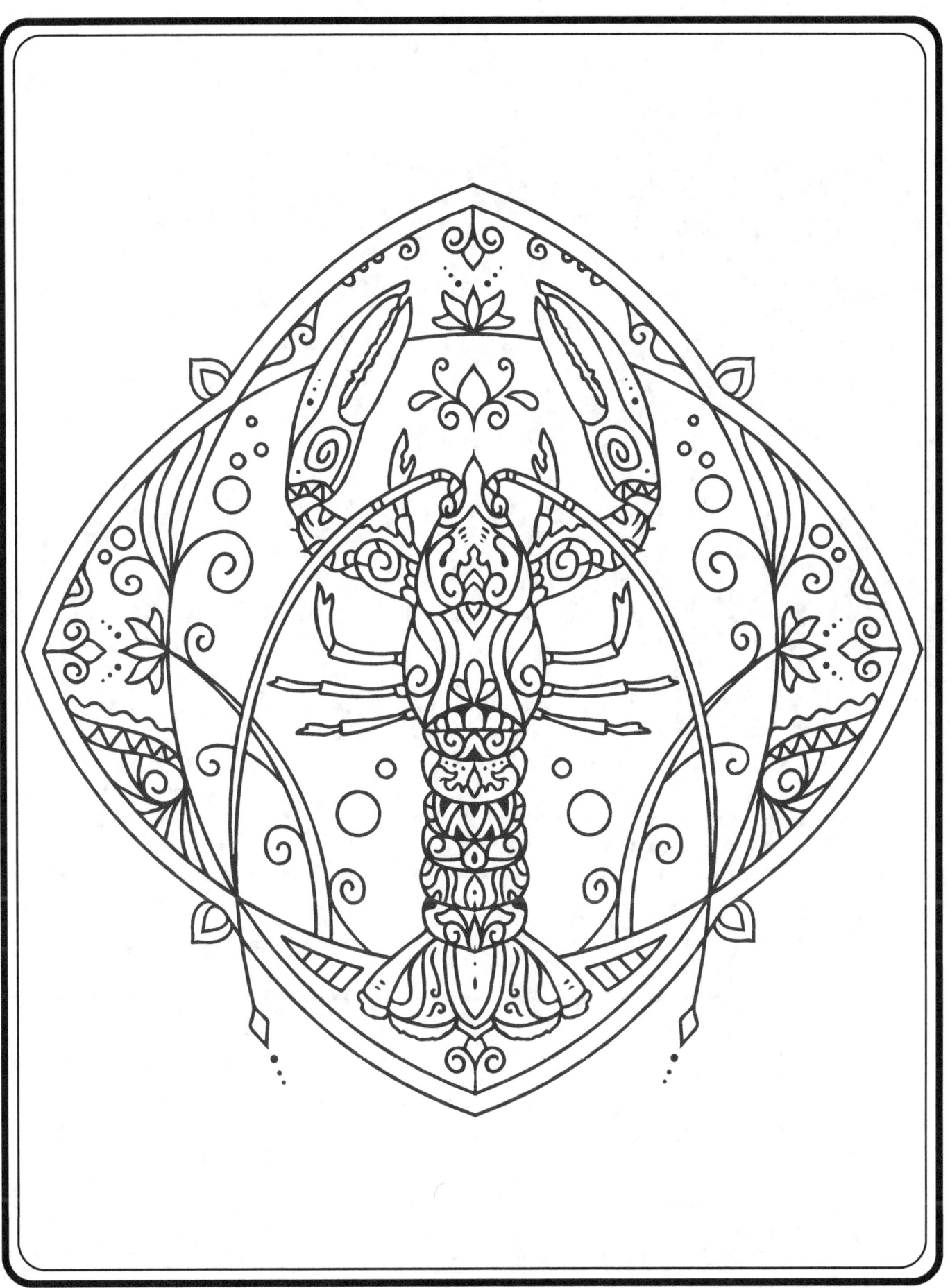

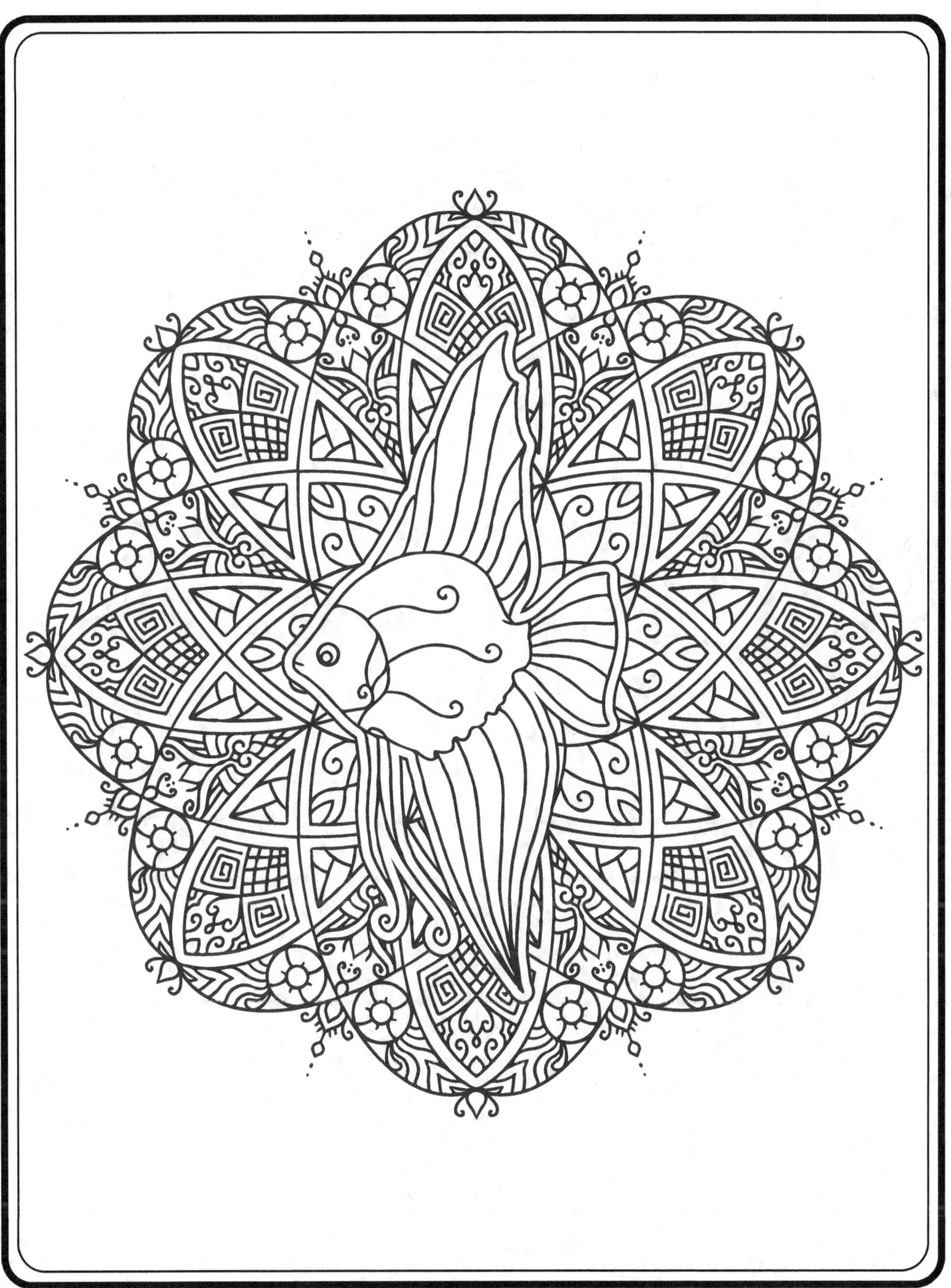

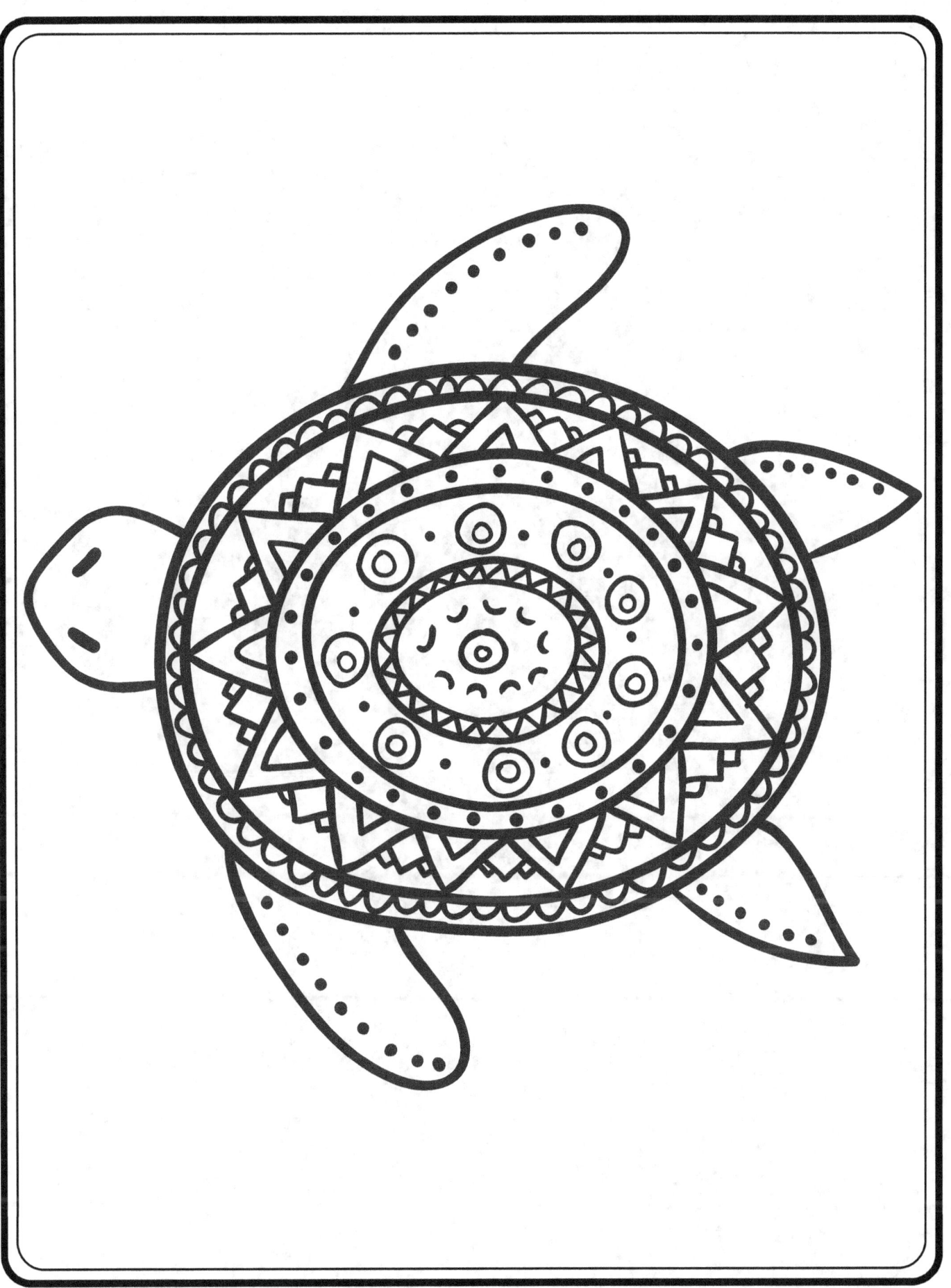

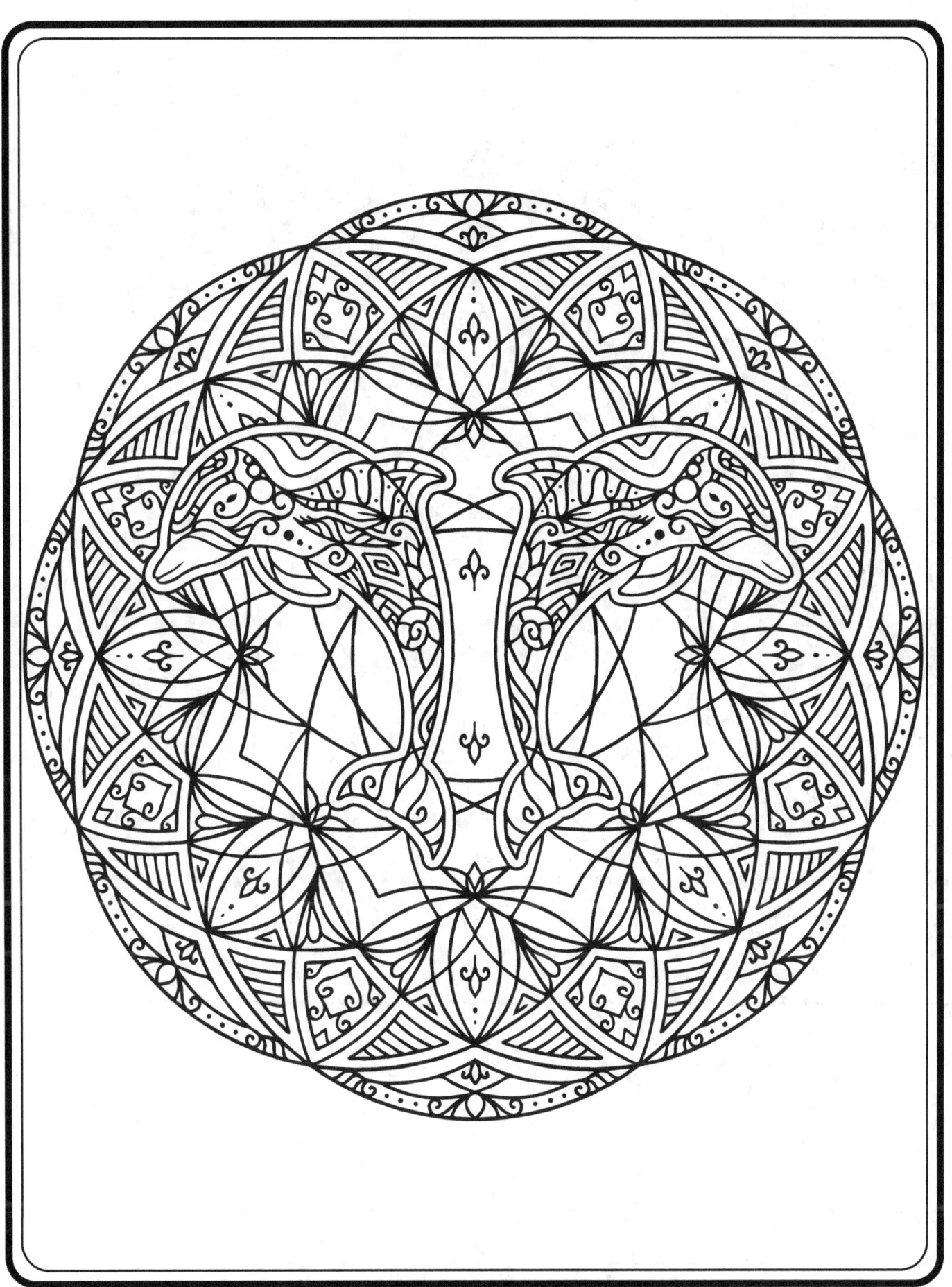

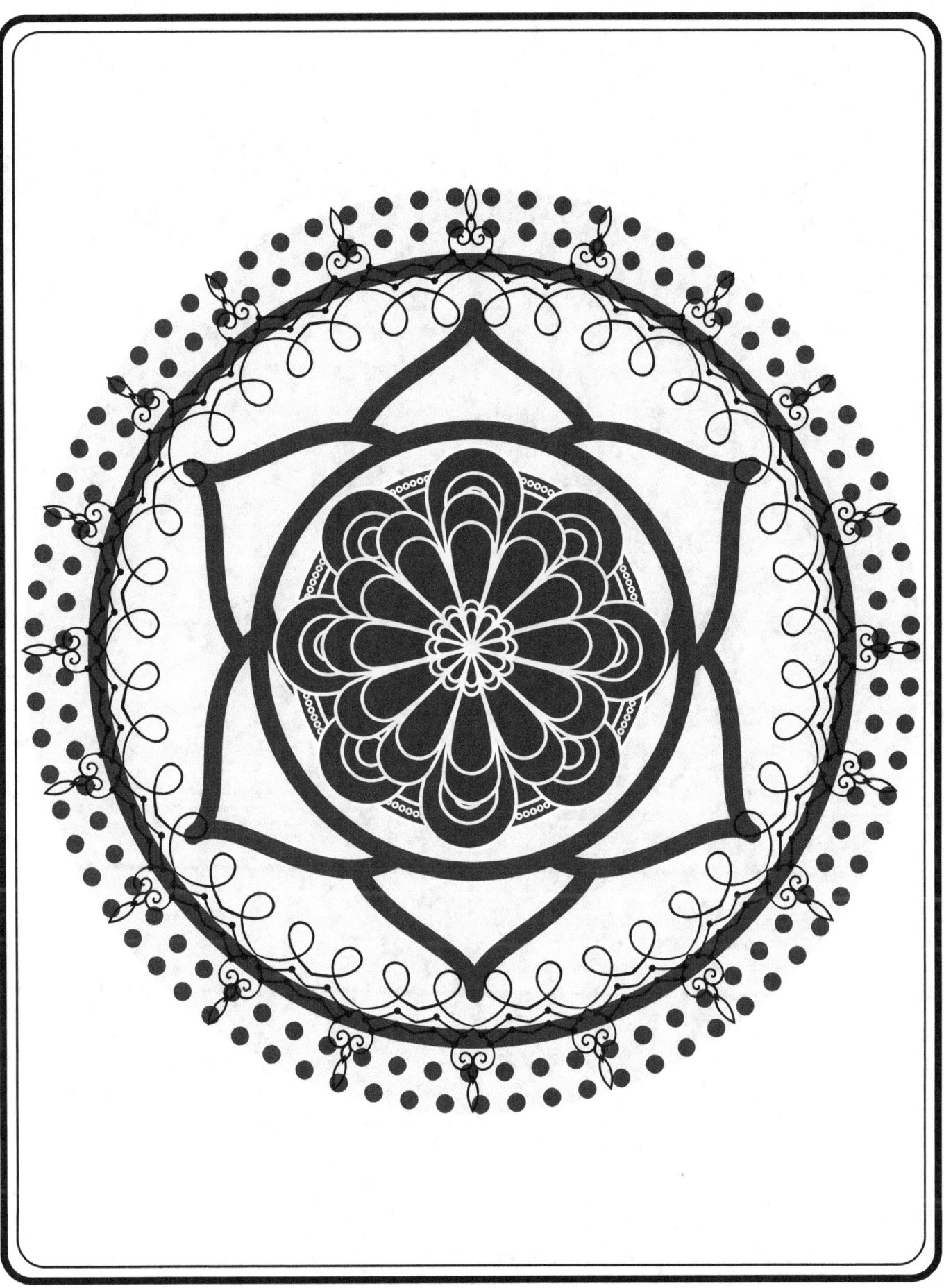

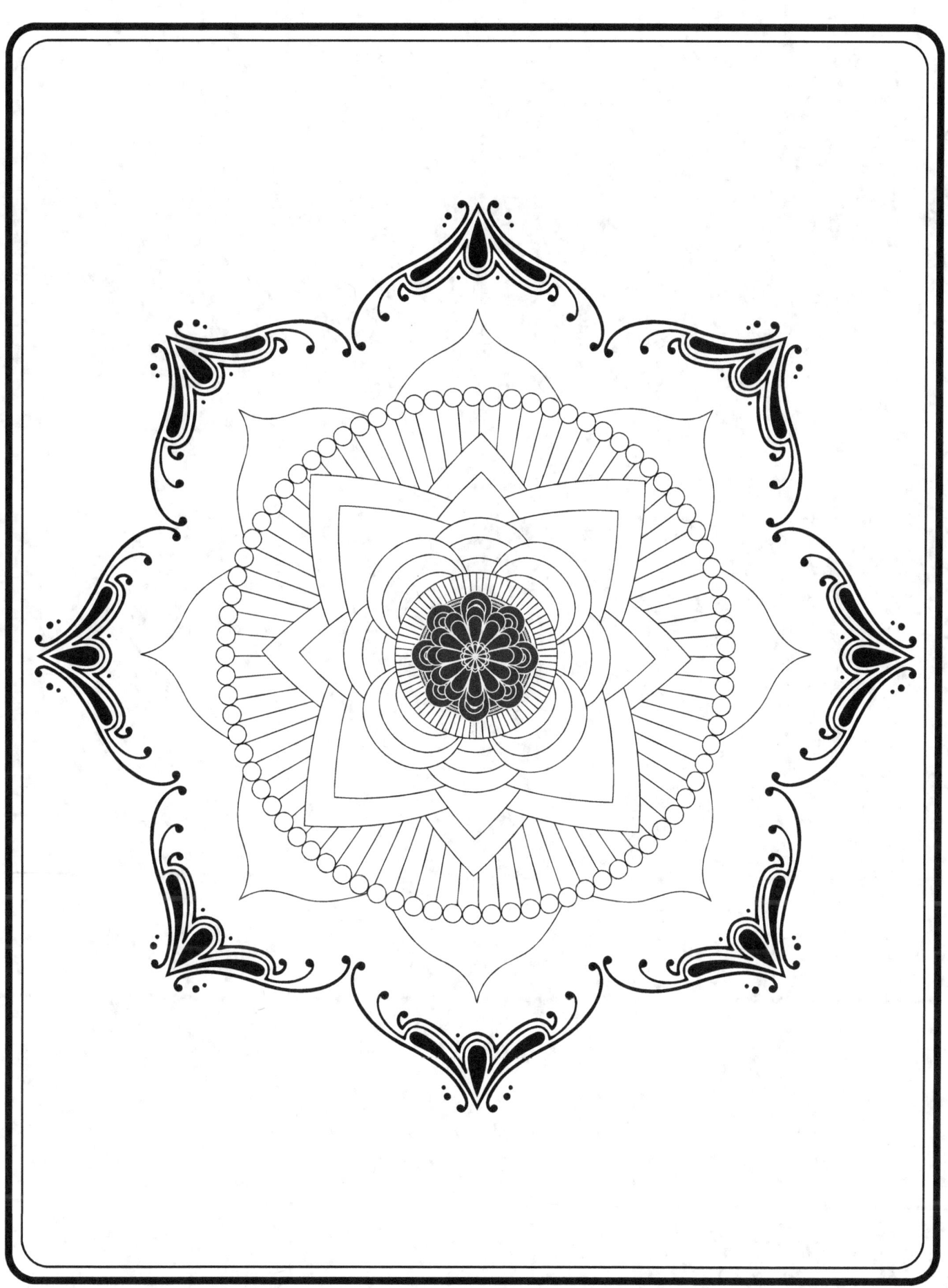

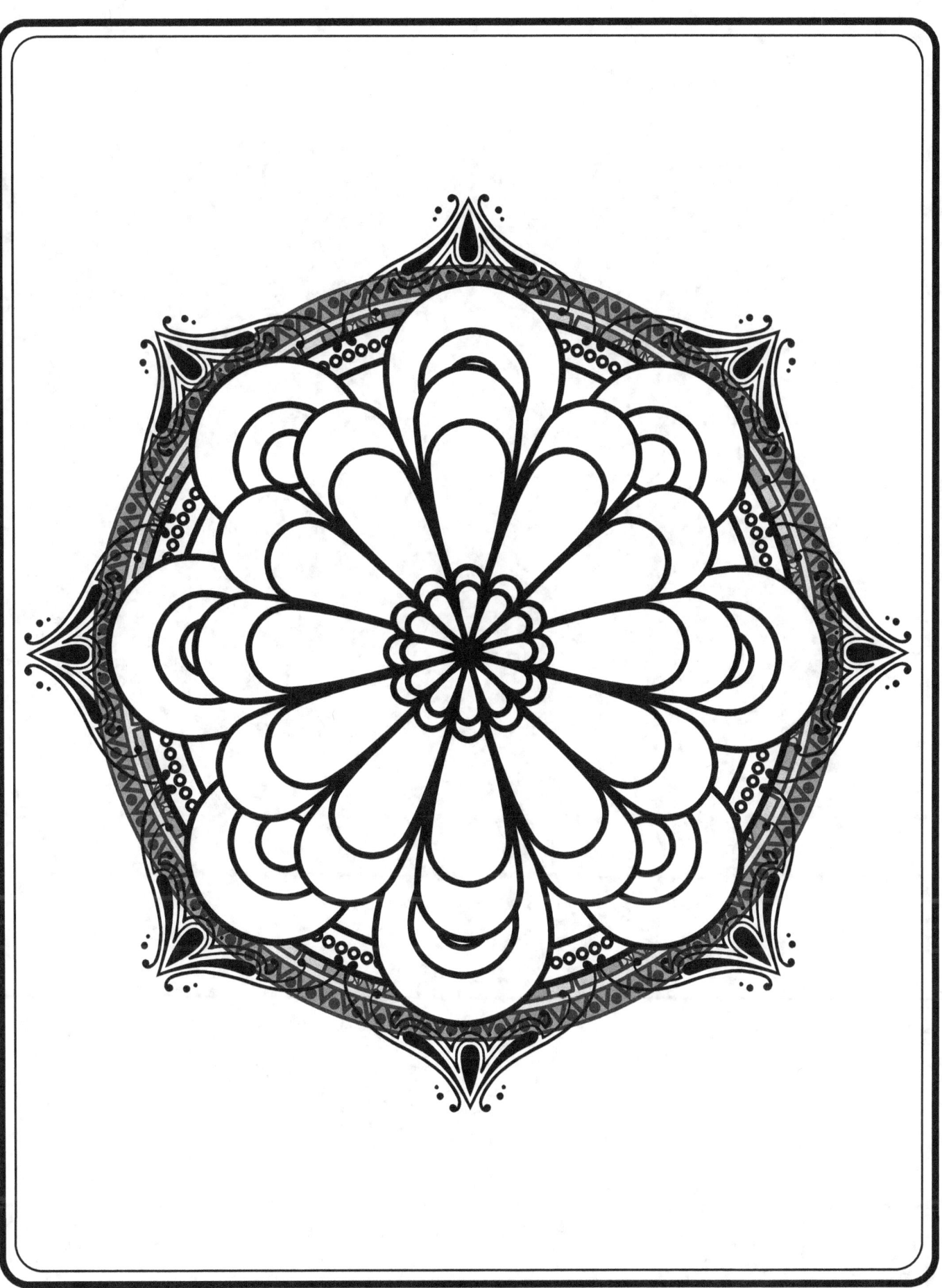

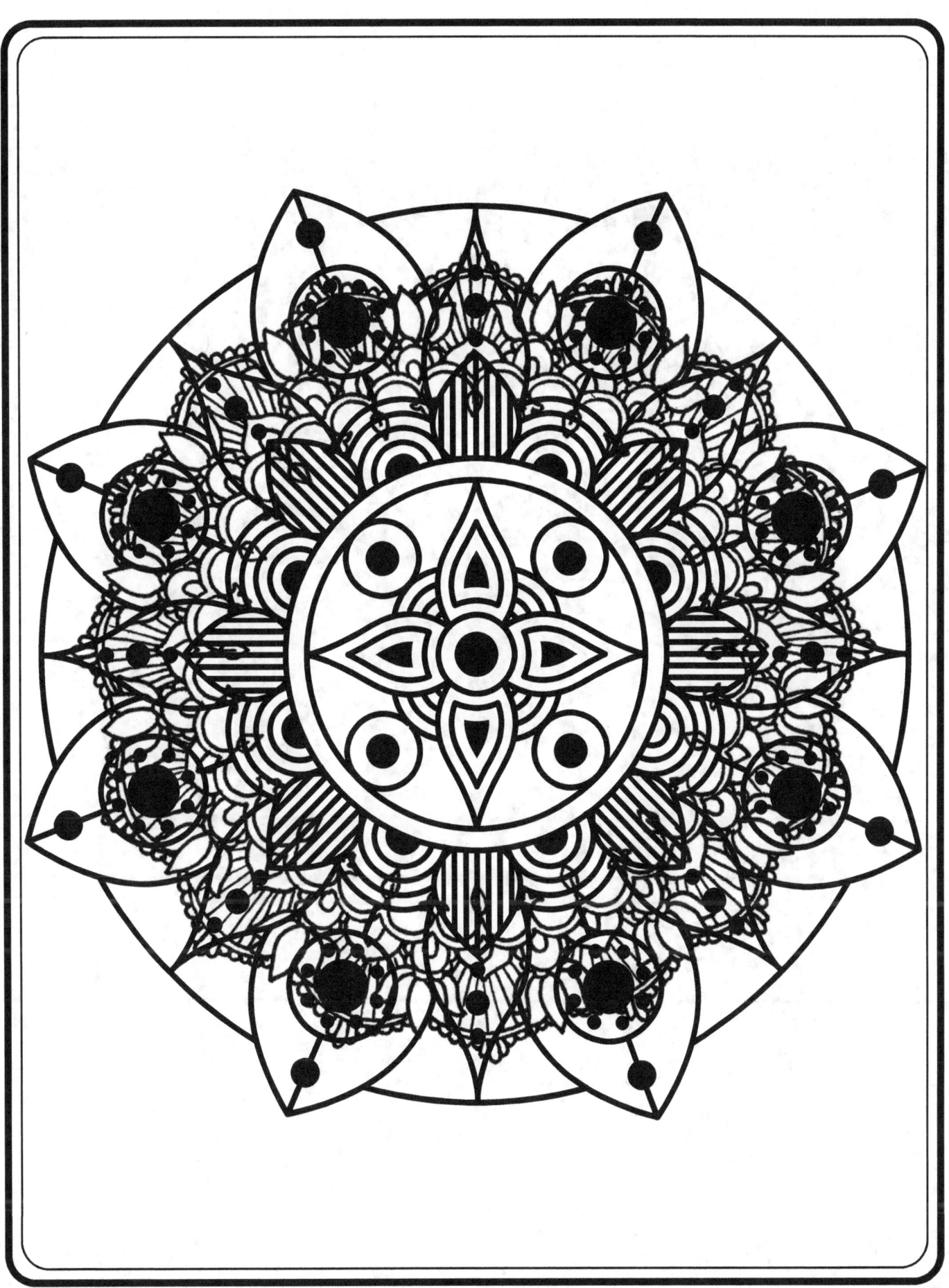

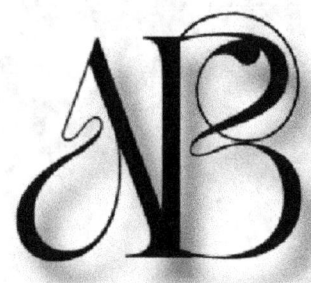

Copyright © 2022 A.B.

www.ingramcontent.com/pod-product-compliance
Lightning Source LLC
Chambersburg PA
CBHW080742240526

45472CB00024B/1766